PRAISE FOR *L*

T0244697

"The daughter of a country m... ... ... and even the topography of her native land in this coming-of-age story of a past she's not always proud of."
—ZIBBY OWENS, *Good Morning America*

"Like listening to a country music song written by Dostoyevsky (lots of crime, but the wrong folks getting punished), with Tom Robbins as his side man. And a little Tennessee Williams thrown in . . . Many a passage of this familial strife and personal coming-of-age chronicle fairly hums on the page, amplified by sharp observation, razor-edge emotion and a delicious turn of phrase . . . A triumph of style as of substance."
—BILL THOMPSON, *The Post and Courier*

"J. Nicole Jones' devastating memoir examines the realities of living in a picture-perfect, privileged family where nothing is as it seems to the public eye."
—K. W. COLYARD, *Bustle*

"Gorgeous, ambling passages that veer from the beach to the bar, from crumbling edifices of lost wealth to secret rooms filled with dolls . . . A tangled memoir told as a tall tale and as true as lived experience . . . It is impossible not to lose yourself in the story of a young, whip-smart girl, who is trying to make sense of this world of men, a world where the best thing women can hope for is to return and haunt the territory."
—HILARY LEICHTER, *Literary Hub*

"A storyteller from a long line of Southern storytellers, Jones forgoes tidy narratives and traditional story arcs . . . With childlike wonder, Jones pulls back the Spanish moss to reveal the swampy muck of her youth and blends it with tall tales, weather reports, history lessons, and family lore in captivating, lyrical prose that carries the reader along like a slow river water park ride on a lazy, sunny day." —SUZANNE VAN ATTEN, *Los Angeles Review of Books*

"Jones' attention to language is what makes this memoir a stunning read . . . At times amusing and other times heartbreaking, her care with language shines through in every page . . . Jones provides a brilliant look into the cracks of a family, channeling the folktales and sayings from her ancestors, and bringing them to the page." —ANITA GILL, *Chicago Review of Books*

"With the prose of a poet, Jones paints a vivid picture of an unorthodox life in an unconventional place." —SUZANNE VAN ATTEN, *The Atlanta Journal-Constitution*

"Jones has succeeded in the role of family archivist, imploring us to see that the story of the Jones family is the story of South Carolina . . . *Low Country* teaches the ways family is born out of place, and the ways we are born out of each other." —RAY LEVY UYEDA, ZYZZYVA

LOW COUNTRY

A Southern Memoir

J. Nicole Jones

Catapult · New York

To Nana & Grandpa

Copyright © 2021 by J. Nicole Jones
First Catapult edition: 2021
First paperback edition: 2024

Hardcover ISBN: 978-1-948226-86-8
Paperback ISBN: 978-1-64622-123-3

Cover design by Robin Bilardello
Cover images: swamp © iStock / SL_Photography; leaves © Shutterstock /
Polina Katritch; snake © Shutterstock / boykotapaint
Book design by Jordan Koluch

Library of Congress Control Number: 2020942085

Printed in the United States of America
1 3 5 7 9 10 8 6 4 2

Contents

Low Country

1

While I Breathe, I Hope

ONCE DOWN IN THE LOW COUNTRY, I SAW THE ghost of a woman I knew well. Not the cool silver specters observed by men that portend danger and violent endings, but a beauty who basked in wide strands of sunshine and predicted nothing but herself. She walked slowly along the shore as if taking in the clear winter sky and soothing song of low-tide surf on the beach that connects the boardwalk with Ocean Boulevard on one side and with the Atlantic on the other. It was the first day of a new year. An easy time to get lost in the portal crease between calendar pages, or any pages, really. Ours is a tourist town alive only half the year at most, and who is to say that spirits do not need a vacation every now and then like the rest of us? She did not see me as she had in life, and I froze breathless, unable to move for equal fear of her attention and her vanishing. I watched this figure as she strolled and smiled, a seductive curving form that might pass for the lolling dunes behind us or the sprawl of waves beyond. She looked in her white pleated shorts and pink bikini top like any other visitor in search of something from our beach to take home. Wherever that might be these days. While I breathe, I hope, says our humble state motto, but surely there is hope for the ghosts of South Carolina too.

I have seen a few such unbelievable occurrences and have heard of many more. Across inlets tinted the lavender gray of looming afternoon storm clouds and marshes fringed green and gold with reedy spartina grass, this coast has entertained the most distinguished of pirates and every sort of sea monster, from mermaids and megalodons to slave ships and surging tempests. Now the history is hidden beneath the plastic indignities of scratchy Astroturf and fiberglass minotaurs that invite tourists to play miles of miniature golf courses, for which the city of Myrtle Beach is distinguished as the world's capital. A selection of historical dinner theater that is awfully forgetful caters to out-of-towners with inelegant accents who come for tans and leave with tattoos. A coast is fundamentally a liminal space, I suppose.

Our family has made its living off the stories and legends of the Low Country since long before my lifetime.

With my brothers and cousins, all sons of sons except for me, I have searched for buried treasure rumored to have been hidden by the pirate Blackbeard under this looking-glass sand. When we did not find it there, we dug up the briny slime of pluff mud at low tide and stalked the pines at the edges of the family's golf courses looking for relics of our history. Under bedsheet tents printed with dinosaurs and aglow in candlelight, my dad and his brother, Uncle Leslie, brought to life sunken galleons, crumbled plantations, and cemeteries haunted by the eternally unfulfilled souls of lonely wives and love-lorn daughters carried away by sea or sickness. Vengeful spirit remains among the main opportunities for ambitious women in the Low Country, and I took note as the boys took cover.

I know several God-fearing folks who claim to have seen with their own eyes the Gray Man pacing the beaches of Pawley's Island before hurricanes Hugo and Hazel. Some will say they've seen him before the lesser unnamed storms of recent years, though any kid here can tell you that is not how it works. If the laws are few and far between in South Carolina, the rules that govern our folklore are kept strict, and any ghost worth her salt respects such soundness. So you see, even as the law has little place here, a crooked logic carries sway. Like many native sons and daughters, the Gray Man rouses for a hurricane, and it is a stroke of luck to be forewarned of approaching danger by whoever he was. Hold your breath when going past a graveyard, unless you want to breathe in a lost and lingering soul. Hang your empty bottles from tree branches to catch a stray evil eye. Paint your ceilings the calm, cool blue of a late-September sky after an almighty storm to trick the haints from coming out at night. It really is a lovely color. What is tradition if not a truce with the unknown, of which there isn't as much as there used to be. Good ghost stories have disappeared as fast as decency in these times. Like a full-moon ocean wave or a tree branch in a hurricane, an authentic one will knock you over the side of the head. A sideways glance is the most graceful escape in the direct path of such forces, though it is a discipline to look away.

I have been gone thirteen years, give or take some superstition. When I return, I tell myself only one story: that this is the last time, and this last time may finally end up as such, if I can look away. My nana, a witty beauty to match any Mitford sister and with more common sense than the bunch, has told me that I talk like a Yankee now. She forgave this ugliness and all the rest. It is only in conversation with her, whose drawl is as deep as her memory, that my own accent creeps out from wherever it lies. Under tongue or heart, depending on mood or drink.

I come from a line of women for whom being walked all over and jumped on for the fun of cruelty was progress. The ironing out of accent was a way to fool myself into believing that I could be different than those women who suffered to make me. If I could have painted the roof of my mouth that lovely shade of haint blue to scare away the ghosts of women I did not want to be, the women I came from, I would have licked clean the brush. I was supposed to be a boy, declared both a doctor and the family tree. It was impressed upon me that I was wanted however I came out, but I have wondered if this aberration rooted in me from the beginning a sense of indignation and unbelonging. The near-miss is a favorite trick of fate, and I always knew that being a girl meant hurting for what my brothers didn't realize they had. Remarking upon this or any injustice was considered rude, I learned fast. My unease did not matter, so long as I was seeing to the ease and comfort of those around me. A lesson I hated to see practiced by my nana and mom, but found myself following.

Nana didn't keep pear trees or hang trinkets from any ancestral cedar, but an ample magnolia stands skyscraper-tall in her backyard. From the top branches, you can see clear across to the beach and back a few centuries. What is now King's Highway, still the main road in town, was once the route George Washington took when he visited Long Bay, as Myrtle Beach was known in 1791, and the road was named in typical backward civility for the new republic's first president. Only once in my lifetime has the tide flirted with the roots of our Great Tree, and no storm has yet knocked it over, so who knows what's up there. Memories woven between branches alongside the other forgotten junk. Swing ropes and water guns and toy action figures. Children are all born pagans, inspired by season, sin, and blood sacrifice.

My parents moved us away from Myrtle Beach when I was in high school, and Charlotte, North Carolina, may as well have been New York City. While my childhood classmates became teenage mothers and drug addicts or both, I was sent home from my fancy college prep school, having applied and tested for admittance as my lone act of teenage rebellion, for wearing overalls. I got made fun of for dressing and talking like the hick I was. In a lonely flashlight-lit blanket tent, I read aloud *Their Eyes Were Watching God* over and over to comfort myself in the more familiar realm of put-upon women who talked in the melodies of my nana, a music that I knew from watching her could cushion the severest of blows. I didn't say much in school, but when I did, it was always the right answer, delivered in perfect television neutral. I was experienced at ignoring greater meanness. Rising above, as Nana would say. The name-calling, classroom hair-pulling, being tripped and pushed in hallways. These were small sufferings and worth the tolerating, if this fancy school helped me to escape a fate as vengeful spirit trapped by the stories I knew by heart. A Myrtle Beach education would not get me where I wanted to go, and though I wasn't sure where that was, I knew that it had to be different and far away.

More than a decade after graduating from the fancy college prep school, during a time of devastating grief, I saw weekly a young woman who called herself a healer. In a railroad apartment in Brooklyn, the walls adorned with her own trinkets of worship, we discussed why I left a safe and salaried magazine job, how my writing progressed or didn't, and the things I tried to keep hidden from everyone else I knew. Our sessions were a relief and a terror. I described ghosts I was not sure I had seen and received knowing nods and leading questions that made me feel, for an hour a week, less alone. Were those really the voices of loved ones long gone who called out my name in subway cars and expensive restaurants and while I brushed my teeth? She held her palms an inch over my navel for long periods or pinched my toes following a particular order, as I held cool white stones of differing shapes that were painted in pretty patterns of smiling suns and dreamy-eyed prancing jaguars. She said these stones were from the Andes, and I felt it impolite to press. "There, you see," she sometimes declared without elaboration after such a performance. More than once, she asked if I knew the tall man with the blue eyes who always stood behind me. One session, she informed me that I had somehow healed all the women I had ever been, as well as all my grandmothers going back to Eve, and I wish that I had asked her how. I began to feel unsettled less by my supernatural company than by her earthside acquaintance. I came to understand what it was I wanted from my own voice and never went back.

The Joneses built their fortune on worshipping the water, before it was lost worshipping wealth. My education was paid for, in part, by tourists who anointed themselves with suntan oil, who glutted themselves annually on deep-fried seafood at all-you-can-eat buffets, readying their own slippery, cooked limbs for sacrifice. With the right SPF, they think they are safe from all manner of natural forces. They don't know which ghosts to watch out for, and we, the locals, take advantage of their ignorance, which makes us blasphemers as well as con men, and I'm just fine with both. Come take a ride on the Ferris wheel that spins like a prayer at the edge of the world, the tallest wheel east of the Mississippi. How easy to feel, in these lofty moments, that this life is more real than the tall tales that outlive the memories and outlast the souvenirs. Don't forget to have some ice cream at Painter's after.

I used to think I learned storytelling from my dad. From the country-music songs he wrote and sang all day and the tall tales of the Low Country that he told us each night. On forests' worth of sunny yellow legal pads, under the sacred porcelain gaze of an Elvis Presley bust looking down from his bookshelf on high, Dad wrote as I sat on the carpet and waited for him to sing and ask, "What do you think, baby?" Between the pirate legends and ghost stories, the fairy tales of my childhood were his verses about bad luck and lonesome women, and I could see the stories become reality in the women I loved but did not want to be like. In the evening hours, my brothers and I filled Mason jars with lightning bugs to keep as night-lights after the candles were blown out so Dad could chase the neon lights of fame, playing low-ceilinged honky-tonks up and down the Carolinas and sometimes into Georgia. When I woke each morning, Dad was always sleeping the deep sleep of whiskey and defeat on the couch with his cowboy boots still on, his guitar in its case by the door, and my lightning bugs upside down with suffocation in the grass at the bottom of their jars. Years later, home from college and about to leave the South for good, I found that Elvis bust in a cabinet. Picking it up for the first time, I saw that it was a bourbon decanter and not a golden calf. That we had been praying to the alcohol all along explained a few things.

I know now that I was already filled with the stories of women. From my mom, I learned how to live with a broken heart, as she knew from hers. Nothing will wreck a marriage like the horizon. Mom tried to anchor Dad to her in all the usual ways a woman tries. Powdered cheekbones, sea-green eyes done up to glitter, auburn hair scorched into mermaid waves. She dressed the part of a country-music star's wife before he was half famous. Fringe, sequins, shoulder pads. Sparkles are a sure sign of magic, and I thought she was more beautiful than Dolly Parton in that skin-tight, hot-pink number from the *Dolly* show. Any costume suited her figure, which even after a litter of kids and a diet of food-stamp fare, retained the perfect and irresistible curves of a guitar. There's nothing so attractive as symmetry. I read somewhere that writing a song is like building a house, which I reckon rings true. Our family has lived in a lot of houses over the years. Only one of them burned down, and most of the guitars made it out all right. A little singed is still fine playing shape.

Dad left us to move to Nashville more than a few times, and he came back every time but one. He spent the 1980s and '90s trying to sell himself to the executives on Music Row, leaving orphan cassette-tape demos tucked inside wicker baskets on their doorsteps. I began telling my own bedtime stories. From Myrtle Beach, he could afford the trip to Tennessee only once or twice a year. While he worked in the family's motels and restaurants, he saw his buddies in Nashville wind up with record deals and writing contracts. He finally chose music over us for good, and after decades of being told he'd never make it, he made it big in what they call outlaw country, the inevitable genre for the descendant of bootleggers and gamblers. Dad and I sang Hank Williams songs to each other in the car, and it is Hank Williams Jr. who sings his songs now. I will tell you that it is disorienting to hear a stranger sing about your life on the radio. Even if we once were the people in those verses, radio always beats reality.

As is Southern tradition, and the premise of most classic country-music duets, my parents separated and reconciled at least a dozen times before and after their divorce. The drinks, the golden rings, and the kids add up to something, but failure pulls on a man's heart stronger than guilt or love. Once he got to Nashville, he'd given himself the ultimate heartache to sing about. He'd lost his family, and I can't let alone the wondering:

Do we have our stories because of the songs? If Dad were not a country-music singer, would there have been all the drinking and the cheating? The violence and the making up? At least the bills might have been paid on time. The South does not own tragedy, but it sure seems to have taken a liking to the region. And why not? The climate's pleasant, and the folks are nice enough to your face. There's an ice machine down the hallway beside the elevator, and pet hermit crabs are ninety-nine cents apiece when you buy a beach towel. I had one I called Periwinkle, and she lived for years in a plastic aquarium filled with little rocks the same synthetic cerulean blue of the water falling from fiberglass rocks at every single mini-golf course. It's true nobody minds her own business, but why would you want to keep quiet when gossip comes with a fat slice of pound cake and a blessing offered to offending hearts.

We'll start with a story about Uncle Jack, because when the mythology's run as dry as the county used to be, there's always one more story about my great-uncle Jack. In 1985, four years before Hurricane Hugo and with three kids under three, my parents moved to Conway, South Carolina, barely inland from Myrtle Beach. Dad was driving to Murrells Inlet to tend bar for the night at Drunken Jack's, named for a different Jack, whom we will get to in due time. He's cruising down Highway 544 in his beat-up pickup truck, the one Hank Williams Jr. sings about getting repossessed on the radio. Just about to the old-fashioned turn-bridge over the Intracoastal Waterway, where the riverboat casino docks, a white Cadillac appears in his rearview mirror, getting closer and closer until the headlights disappear into his bumper, and he is run off the road. In a cloud of dust and mosquitos—so mad he doesn't even bother to check for water moccasins, as he taught us to do so close to the water—Dad jumps out of the car with more than cussing on his mind. "What in the hell do you think you're doin'?" he starts to yell. You see, he knows the car and its driver. His uncle, Jack Jones, looks at him from behind the wheel and smiles. "Mark, get in the car" is all he has to say. Getting in the car with Jack means conceding to a trip over state lines and possibly breaking at least state, if not federal laws, according to nearly every story passed around the family. Dad protests at first, but there's not much use in saying no to Jack. He can't lose his job, he says. He can't leave Debbie alone with the kids, he says. He's broke and doesn't have any business leaving the county, he says. And what is he supposed to do with his truck? "Jack was the most fun, but I hated to see his face at the door," Mom will remember now.

In this scene, Jack is dressed like one of the gangsters people said he knew. A friend of my dad's, on seeing Jack around town wearing a large gold medallion and nothing else for a shirt, said to him in the utmost seriousness, "I didn't know your uncle was in the Olympics." When Jack runs you off the road and says get in the car, well, there really isn't anything to do except leave your own truck where it is on the side of the road and get in the car. So Dad climbs into the Cadillac, and notes, for storytelling purposes, the velour tracksuit with the jacket's zipper wide open to show off the gold medallion that hangs atop his rolls of opulent, browned fat and the coils of more gold chains piled around his neck. Jack made more money than just about anybody in Myrtle Beach and didn't have to get up out of his recliner to do it, they say. In his obituary, Jack is described as "having a financial mind like no other," which could not be argued with. Among his closest friends, continues the newspaper, was a state Supreme Court justice called Bubba.

"Where are we going?" Dad asks a few times, and on the south side of Georgetown, ninety minutes past Conway, Jack finally answers.

"We're going to Miami." He elongates his words even more than usual for emphasis, letting the last *i* in Miami pull up the corners of his Cheshire grin. When Mom answers the phone, barefoot on our parquet kitchen floor, she knows right away from my dad's tone. "Lord, you didn't get into the car with Jack, did you?"

Jack drives them down to a casino in Florida that he is thinking of buying. He is always thinking of buying a casino in Florida. They hole up in a couple of motel rooms for a week, and my dad is a very well-kept hostage who's probably not having that bad a time as they drink, gamble, and flirt their way in the general direction of Cuba. One morning a week or so into their road trip, Dad decides that enough is enough, he wants the car keys or a bus ticket home. He finds his uncle's motel-room door unlocked, creeps past the bed where Jack and a young lady who is not his wife are asleep. He starts pawing at pants pockets and opening drawers looking for Jack's keys or his wallet. Eventually, he notices something else of value beside the nightstand lamp. "Jack," he says as he kicks the bed, which jiggles all manner of flesh let loose during the course of the night. "You either give me some cash for a bus ticket home, or you ain't never gonna see your teeth again." At this he holds aloft the set of pink-and-white dentures swiped for ransom.

"You'd steal the teeth out of your own family's mouth?" Jack said, remembers my dad.

To which he replied, Dad recollects, and here it is my turn to repeat those words in no less an act of outright theft, "It's time for me to go home."

2

Treasure Maps

AT THIS MOMENT, WE ARE PULLING BACK THE tangled kudzu curtains on 1979 to set the scene for my parents to meet so that I might appear. Live oaks sprawl, and Spanish moss seeps from their gray limbs into the watercolor pastels of a vacation sunset. A salty ocean breeze surfs the sour marsh air beside the tang of margarita mix blended with summer sweat and spit laced with snuff on the back patio of a new bar in Murrells Inlet named for the pirate Drunken Jack. Cigarette smoke coils like fat water moccasins around branches of groping hands and through wisps of feathered hair. It is not impossible that a boat smuggling cocaine has just unloaded straight from Escobar's equatorial empire due south, after a journey that skirted the Atlantic's seasonal squalls and a final cruise to safety through the labyrinth of rice fields abandoned but for the alligators and tidal islands that lie in wait under black marsh water to strand outsiders who don't know where to round a bend or skirt a sandbar. The boat might pass Sandy Island, the Gullah community descended from the enslaved Africans who labored the surrounding rice plantations. Let us imagine the captain of this unnamed vessel pulling from his pocket a book of matches designed with an image of Drunken Jack, the smiling, one-eyed pirate, on the back flap. Drunken Jack's was where you went to find all kinds of treasure.

Like a decent portion of the population, I owe my existence to a bar. My parents met at an upscale Calabash seafood joint off Restaurant Row on King's Highway in that sticky, druggy summer of 1979, as it is recalled. Dad was the twenty-year-old bartender, born and raised in Myrtle Beach, the youngest son of a family of sons and brothers who owned a portion of the motels, pancake houses, golf courses, and other assorted tourist traps in Horry County. Mom was a waitress, the new girl in a small town who had both beauty-queen looks and novelty to her advantage. Debbie Allen had dropped out of her all-girls' community college in Raleigh, North Carolina, with her roommate, a woman who would become known to us kids in cruel awe as the Black Widow, after the untimely, strange, and varied deaths of several young husbands. Debbie and her friend set up in an apartment whose bamboo furniture

and seashell motifs were evidence to them, as to all inland emigrants, that the fantasy of the beach holiday
exists as daily life for coastal residents. They waitressed
together first at a diner in Cherry Grove, a strip of inlet beach south of a rusty swing bridge that crosses the
same Intracoastal Waterway where farther down the
county in Socastee Uncle Jack will kidnap my dad in a
few years.

Mom knew Cherry Grove from childhood vacations with her father, when a post–Korean War boom
in middle-class vacationing coincided with a post–
Hurricane Hazel construction boom and all-around re-
drawing of the coastline in 1954. Maps you've used your
whole life no longer work after big hurricanes. A rickety
pier, bait shops, and ice-cream parlors popped up where
only crab traps and widows' walks had been before in
the coastal village north of Myrtle Beach. Henry Allen
named his three daughters after movie stars and his only
son after himself, as blind to his own vanity as most
men. Over six feet tall, blond and blue-eyed himself, he
had the kind of good luck that makes you wonder if
certain gods still play patron to their favorites, and lived
at a time when his right to be the best at everything
could never be questioned. He talked his way around a
story as well as Odysseus, and Southern spirits rewarded
his gifts with fortune more valuable than, but certainly
including, gold. His wife, my mother's mother, was no
pining Penelope, though. She could not resist her suitors
and had exiled herself to her own island far away by the

time Henry was taking his four kids to Cherry Grove for summer weekends.

At the end of these holidays, Henry was perennially unable to wrestle his eldest daughter into the car. There was nothing to do but wait for her to finish splashing and swimming, and then return soaking, sunbaked, and happy in her own good time for a four-hour drive through pine forests, tobacco fields, and peach trees back to the red-clay dirt of Charlotte. Something called to her out beyond the surf. Again I imagine her a mermaid with a tail the same green as her eyes, as I recall the unquestionable existence of mermaids verified in a classroom text, but my schooling is not a part of the story just yet. Around this same time, right around the early 1960s, my dad and his tribe of brothers and cousins would have been diving for sand dollars and conch shells, which they sold for a dollar apiece to old Mrs. Plyler at the Gay Dolphin, for decades billed as the nation's "largest gift shop" in slanted cursive over Ocean Boulevard. Were they ever in the water at the same moment as children, I wonder, and on the page, I'm inclined toward synchronicity over sense.

Things were going along according to plan, as they usually are before they aren't. Mom was counting her tips and enjoying life in general as a full-time vacationer. The Chesapeake House used to offer a view of the ocean over the marsh. Now the restaurant's windows are filled by high-rise time-shares and stucco-plastered hotels. The restaurant has never had a view of the Chesapeake, that famous bay several states to the north, though it has always been a house and remains done up like a farm, painted in red with white trim. Curtains of matronly lace shade the windows behind the fake Tiffany stained-glass lamps that hang over the bar. The night my parents met, the brackish water may have teased a syrupy shade of dark red wine underneath all that moonlight. It would have been particularly beautiful then, and even the alligators between the reeds would seem under the spell of backwater charm.

I'd like to pretend, though, that they met at a different bar. One that plays a more consistent role in my family's history. With permission, we'll relocate this scene to Drunken Jack's. The view's better and the drinks are stronger. Such a well-meaning and convenient move puts us closer to the Grand Strand tradition of laying claim to obscurities. At least I'm being upfront with you. How many of the juke joints along the boardwalk claiming to be the "birthplace of the shag" couldn't tell you the steps to dance? Forward, to the side, and back till you're spinning. We must place our feet in the right pattern, in the right time, so the memories can turn into history and the future might hurt a little less from its past.

Drunken Jack's opened up in the late 1970s, when Mom moved to the beach, and both my parents wound up working there for longer, anyway. "I still have dreams of polishing the wood on the captain's wheel," Mom said the last time we were at Drunken Jack's, as we walked past its glossy spokes and down the paisley-carpeted stairs into the dining room that looks over Murrells Inlet. As kids, my brothers and I dressed in our parents' old uniform T-shirts of teal blue or pale yellow with the matchbook depiction of Drunken Jack himself on the front and the back. Stained and threadbare, they were a glamorous connection to the most famous pirate of all.

It is a fact that in the late 1600s and into the next century, Blackbeard wore out the *Queen Anne's Revenge* ransacking the Carolina coast and then pulling into the inlets around Horry County to hide out. I remember Little River as not much more than a swing bridge, some aboveground pools, boat docks, and roadside fireworks stands, but the town's history hides as well as any treasure still buried. It is one of the oldest settlements in South Carolina. Right below the North Carolina border, it was, in Blackbeard's day, the only stop between Cape Fear and Georgetown, and the lone entrance to the undesirable and difficult-to-navigate Long Bay, which was basically the whole stretch of Horry County then. Edward Teach was not the only pirate who favored the hazards of the Low Country for hiding out. Blackbeard's friend Charles Vane so vexed the merchants of Charleston by stealing their cargo ships coming into port, including ships carrying enslaved Africans, that they engaged privately the pirate-hunting services of a William Rhett, a rice planter and naval commander whose house still stands peachy pink on Hasell Street in Charleston, smack between the City Market built in 1790 and a Harris Teeter grocery mart. Black Bart, who captured as many as four hundred ships and is considered the most successful pirate by the standard of vessels seized, is said to have worn a pluming red feather in his hat during raids. Black Bart is not to be confused with Black Sam Bellamy. Bellamy called himself the Robin Hood of the Sea and is accounted by many as the richest pirate ever to sail, said to have fallen in love with the Witch of Wellfleet and been claimed nonetheless by a hurricane.

Then there is Stede Bonnet, the genteel English aristocrat who supposedly became a pirate to escape his nag of a wife. He was known as the Gentleman Pirate, but never sounded very gentlemanly to me. All in all, Mrs. Bonnet seemed better off without him. Bonnet tried to befriend Teach, having some things in common, but Teach caught on to Bonnet's bungling, took him prisoner, and stole his ship and crew. Blackbeard decided that Bonnet was more trouble than he was worth and let him go, while he holed up in Little River. Bonnet was not a very good pirate and was soon caught by the rice planter Rhett, though he managed to escape his jailers by dressing as a high-society lady and walking straight out of the Charleston house where he was held, the story goes. So little have South Carolinians thought of the law, there was no jail across the state well into the 1770s, a full century and a half after the founding of the Charles Towne colony. Aristocratic prisoners were treated as guests in the house of the local lawmen. South Carolinians have long delighted in the words of the statesman James Petigru, from just before the Civil War. "South

Carolina is too small for a nation and too large for an insane asylum." Petigru was ridiculed as the only man in the state who decried secession and supported the Union. I wonder if some residents would be so quick to quote Petigru if they knew he had been a Unionist.

Between hideouts in Little River, Blackbeard absconded on some adventure with more rum than his trusty galleon could keep afloat. The crew diverted the *Revenge* to a little island off the coast of Murrells Inlet, where they proceeded to bury the extra casks of rum and gold, feast on whatever seventeenth-century pirates feasted on, probably not what the tourists are fed at Pirate's Voyage Dinner Show on Restaurant Row, where the Dixie Stampede used to be, and celebrate their bountiful, boozy good fortune. Come sunrise, in a hurry to catch the tide or to get their hangovers out of the sun, the band of pirates forgot to do a head count and set sail one pirate short. By the time they realized Jack was missing, Blackbeard was halfway to Aruba and unwilling to turn the ship around. They came back six months or six years later to find all their rum dug up and Jack's bare, sun-bleached bones under a palmetto tree, surrounded by jewels and empty casks. You can see Drunken Jack's island from the bar named for him. It's called Goat Island these days, as locals used to cart over a family of goats in the summertime to eat the marijuana plants that grow so happily in our climate. In the interest of history, I must disclose that there is another story. That the island is named for a drunk who belonged to a gentle-

men's club of secret repute that met on the island as one
of several roaming locations. They'd drink champagne,
catch fish for the enslaved to clean and cook and serve to
them. I have always preferred one story over the other.

A fishing boat ride inland from Goat Island, at
Drunken Jack's, Dad was a bartender with a guitar
and a few ideas about getting famous, and Mom was
filling orders for hush puppies and piña coladas. Dad
already had a reputation in the county as a guy who
went through girlfriends like packs of cigarettes. The
establishments stretching the length of King's Highway
from Little River to Georgetown County were owned or
managed by the Joneses at the time, and Dad had just
moved out of Uncle Jack's house, where he'd lived since
high school, and into a beachy done-up condo with his
two older brothers, Mike and Leslie. "I just couldn't get
along with my old man," Dad will say when he's in a soft
mood, talking a maze around the brutality his father let
flood the house.

That Ralph Cooper Jones, Granddaddy as we call
him, emerges here villainous cannot be helped. The ad-
vantages of femininity are few in Horry County, and I
didn't question when graces fell instead of his blows. Perhaps he didn't know how to handle a girl child—weren't
our bodies supposed to be more delicate? Our worth as
the bearers of sons to be preserved?—and I watched my
brothers and our first cousins, as good as more brothers,
get a belt across their backs every evening when he came
home from his office. A belting was a regular part of the

day, and we, as children aware only of what we could count on, took such strikes for granted, as normal as afternoon thunderstorms or breakfast cereal, which didn't mean the hurt wasn't adding up. We were too young to know what to do with the rage that bloomed under bruises. The first time I saw Granddaddy slap Nana across the face, at four or five, I knew that I hated him, but did not yet know how this baptismal spark of anger bonded us, how it would make me like him, and how it had done the same to my dad. As passively as catching a cold, his disease was activated in my blood, which was partly his, after all.

By the time they were in elementary school, Dad and his brothers were experienced busboys at any number of restaurants along King's Highway. Alcohol was halfway illegal in the 1960s in South Carolina and not allowed served in restaurants, but Uncle Leslie recalls making drinks at a bar hidden in the kitchen of the Hawaiian Village. This tropical-themed restaurant-resort on Highway 17 and Thirty-ninth Avenue was managed by Uncle Jack and owned then by his eldest brother, Keith. Guests were invited to "lose your worries in a carefree Polynesian atmosphere," part of which was the waitresses in grass skirts and coconut bras. The Myrtle Beach police were said to let Keith and Jack know that a raid was on the books for the Hawaiian Village and that they should expect half a dozen men in uniforms ironed neatly and badges shining. After finding only the Coca-Cola and tap water of good Christians on the floor, these men supposedly placed their own drink orders. Waiting in the kitchen were their mai tais and gin fizzes, handed out by only the prettiest waitresses.

Uncle Jack married the best-looking waitress they had at the Hawaiian Village. Betty was tall with unruly curls as black as Jack's. That she could hold Jack's attention was saying something, especially in the Bora Bora room, where hula dancers wearing orchid crowns blew kisses from the stage and shirtless men threw firesticks to one another in streamers of orange afterglow. The night Jack met Betty, Dad and Uncle Leslie were restocking the bar and cleaning tables as if it were any other night, until a guest pulled a gun out of his suit jacket and held it over the room. Dad remembers ducking under a table with an armful of dirty dishes.

"Why'd you go and marry a woman who's gonna talk back to you?" the Jones brothers queried their baby brother, fearing that Aunt Betty's unladylike demands, like fidelity and daughters, might influence their own wives' expectations. Their wives did what a good wife was supposed to do, which is what she was told. Betty was not afraid to interfere, and spoke her mind to all the Jones brothers. When Nana dared talk back to Granddaddy, the best that could happen would be a low rumble, "You've been around Betty, I can tell." Jack and Betty let my dad move in with them as a teenager, after he couldn't live with his father anymore and took off. Uncle Jack saw something of himself in my dad, another youngest son with the instinct natural performers have for getting away with things on a cocktail of charm and indifference. He saw the bruises, too. Born nearly a decade later than the rest of his five brothers, Jack managed to escape his father's temper and could give some safety to his nephew. It only takes the faith of one person to bring about a little peace. "My daddy'd let his sons starve before he'd give away a nickel," Dad has said over and over.

When it was time for Dad to move out of Jack and Betty's place, his brothers Mike and Leslie, blond and blue-eyed like Nana, welcomed their dark-headed baby brother, along with his guitar and his shaggy mutt, into their condo on Ocean Boulevard and Thirty-third Avenue. Dad has always connected to dogs easily and with authority, as wounded animals who recognize each other. Stray dogs would follow him home from school as a boy, and when Dad struck up a particular friendship with one and tried to keep it in the backyard, instead of "good night" or "sleep well," never mind bedtime-story forts, Granddaddy would say as he fell asleep, "I'm gonna kill that dog in the morning." Dad got up early enough as a busboy for breakfast crowds even during the school year to hide his pets at first light, saving scraps of tourists' bacon and pancakes to feed them. Not a penny of the household money was allowed on dog food, until Nana, in a burst of either defiance or loneliness, brought home the first in a series of tiny teacup poodles.

Dad acquired Ghost serendipitously and by accident, when a dog leapt into the car through the open passenger door. He was big enough to fill the whole seat, and they couldn't entice him to jump out. Leaving the windows down, Dad said, "If he's still in the car when we get back, I'm keeping him." He was and so earned his name for materializing out of thin air.

As this was in Columbia, the state capital, they would not have been far from the swamp chestnut trees and old-growth cherrybark oaks of the piedmont where some say resides the ghost of a black, shaggy dog just known as the Hound. In most renderings, he will give chase to lonely walkers late at night, but this particular tale has always seemed too skeletal for my tastes. Ghost stayed with my dad for many years. They took long road trips and went deep-sea fishing. They took a johnboat to the tip of Sullivan's Island, next to Fort Sumter, and rode the elevator to the top of the tetrahedron lighthouse locals call the Charleston Light. It was built in rare modern style in the years after Hazel to withstand the gusts of future hurricanes. From there, Dad and Ghost caught sight of the older lighthouses at Cape Romain a few miles up the coast. Under the water between these sentries lie the remains of the *Planter*, the steamship overtaken and liberated by the enslaved people onboard in 1862. After the Confederate dolts in charge disembarked for a night of drinking, an enslaved deckhand named Robert Smalls put on a captain's uniform and sailed past the Southern watch posts, straight through to the safety of the Union blockade offshore. He freed himself, his family, and the whole crew, and the *Planter* sailed from then on for Lincoln. It sank during a storm a decade later, after delivering cotton to Georgetown, well into Smalls's term as a congressman for South Carolina. Driving down Highway 17 one afternoon with Ghost, Dad was rear-ended and rammed into the car in front of him. He blacked out and woke concussed to a trucker shaking him and offering to take him to the hospital. "Just take me home," he said, but then could not recall where that was. They drove 'round and 'round a neighborhood that seemed sort of familiar, and on the third or fourth time that Ghost barked with urgency in front of one house, the truck driver said, "I think this is where you live, son." The dog disappeared just as he'd shown up in the first place. Ghost's is a better story than the Hound's.

By the time Dad and Ghost were living with his brothers, Mike and Leslie were very nearly full-time gamblers, paying the rent playing cards and tending bar. Perhaps wanting his own fearsome hound, my uncle Leslie responded one day to an ad in the *Sun-Times*. TIMBER WOLF FOR SALE. After driving eight hours to Rock Hill and back, half the time with a wolf in the back seat, it turned out that the wolf had more sense than my uncle and didn't care much for his or anybody else's company. In fact, he didn't care at all for being pent up in a beachside condo and spent his days and nights pacing the floor and snarling at anyone dumb enough to think about coming into the bedroom where they kept him. Les threw a piece of raw chicken at him from the doorway twice a day for a few weeks, before some other kid took him away to let him loose in the swamps around Conway. Perhaps his descendants have joined the Hound or Ghost to wander the pine forests that connect the marshland to the jade tobacco fields, before the soil turns to terra-cotta red in the piedmont that yearns upward toward lush, wild Appalachia, though I'd be more scared of snakes than wolves in a Southern fairy tale.

The boys had all spent their early years in the back rooms of Granddaddy's first motel, a squat two-story concrete affair painted gray and white on the beach side of Ocean Boulevard, much like the other motor lodges that sprang up in the 1950s. Sticking out like a hitchhiker's thumb above the sidewalk, an Atomic Age sign of a blonde mid swan dive in a red bathing suit offered THE SEA DIP like an afterthought in Space Age Filmotype. They'd all been put to work as soon as they could talk and knew well the routines of life on the beach. They'd hop between restaurants bartending and tending the arcade games and waiting tables and stripping hotel sheets as needed, taking their cues from calls from uncles and cousins who owned every other establishment in town. As they earned only their keep from working for their father, they'd sometimes make fast cash in card games or other gambles, like diving for sand dollars as children and later dabbling in cocaine that continued its speedboat delivery from South America. They knew, as all young people from tourist traps inevitably discover, that getting high is the fastest and surest way of getting out of town.

Back at Drunken Jack's, where we agreed to meet earlier, my parents' love story, like all good ones, begins with an act of persuasion. Having been warned of his reputation by the hostess, a former waitress at the Hawaiian Village, Debbie refused the advances of the smooth-talking, dark-haired bartender. Between the aquarium on one side, babbling its unnatural shades of blue and bobbing with imported fish the bright oranges and yellows of drowned plastic mini-golf balls, and the waist-high stage on the other, she turned him down every night as she put in her drink orders. What started as an attraction became an opportunity to perform. Their relationship started on a stage, which is what they had both been waiting for without knowing it. As all young people do, my parents took their youth for specialness, believing that they deserved to be discovered by the world at large, and where fame hadn't yet found my dad in South Carolina, love shone a spotlight instead. To be noticed and loved for nothing but being yourself is an attainable acclaim. Adoration elevates our opinion of ourselves. As it should, my nana would say. Love lets you expect more even when you've got less, and what didn't they expect once they got together.

Have you seen it coming? How he won over the prettiest waitress this side of the Waccamaw? He wrote her a song. He set up a microphone, threw down some carnations, tied some balloons to the light fixtures in his brothers' apartment, and sang a song written about her and crooned only for her ears. Les had gotten rid of the timber wolf by then, and they had the place to themselves. It is a truth that my brothers and I grew up acknowledging as universal that a stage always means success. He had yet to transition from baseball cap to cowboy hat, from Converse to cowboy boots, and sang from the heart. Mom found the lyrics scribbled on a torn-out sheet of notebook paper that was rolled up, tucked inside a wooden jewelry box alongside a mood ring gone a final shade of verdigris, some pocket change, a guitar pick, and a book of matches. Most treasure maps don't ever get found. Just like in the movies, when she discovered this one almost forty years after it was last seen, the paper had ambered with age and frayed along the edges. Old ink bled the bridges into the chorus, but Drunken Jack's matchbook portrait smiled still at the love song written on an aging telescope of paper.

3

*Horse Thieves &
Millionaires*

NOW THAT I AM HALFWAY ON THE SCENE, WE'LL
continue our study of historic documents forgotten inside closets, shoeboxes, coat pockets, and photo albums,
among which I include love notes, grocery lists, records
of sale, old pictures with those wavy edges, lapsed cal-
endars, diaries with years embossed in gold at the bottom right corner of the cover, birthday cards, and fast
scribbles across the back of my hand. Let us pull from
one such shoebox a photograph of the Gay Manor
Hotel, which started it all for the Joneses. A postcard
from 1948 in shades of black and gray shows what must
have been a white brick building of three stories between

Ocean Boulevard, on the south end, and the Atlantic. "670 Miles South of New York, 735 Miles North of Miami" reads a corner of the card, whose parking lot is filled with old, curvaceous black cars. Today it is a pizza parlor in the shadow of the SkyWheel, and a history book says it was started by the Jones brothers, but really it was their father, Harvey, from whom they bought it after World War II. The brothers old enough had all served in the Navy. Harvey Jones had traveled all over doing odd jobs and construction, pulling small-time scams and bootlegging to support his family of sons and one daughter. After they were married, Nana's mother said every chance she could, "There weren't any millionaires on our side of the family, but there weren't no horse thieves neither."

The Joneses settled in Myrtle Beach from Cool Spring, South Carolina, twelve miles north of Conway and east of Dog Bluff. The money for their first hotel built in the 1930s, one of the first on Ocean Boulevard, came from a gas station run by Harvey's wife, my great-grandmother Pearl, only ever called Ol' Mama and acknowledged as the boss. She ran the backroom dealings at the Gay Manor Hotel and the gas station and everywhere else they managed to acquire. Gambling houses and poker dens. Rum-running and burlesque joints. I have only ever seen two photos of her. One in black and white standing unsmiling in a white shirt and black skirt to the floor beside her husband. The second is in color, but tinged the red of photographs from de-

cades past. It's from a baby shower, my mom and Uncle
Leslie's wife each pregnant with another Jones boy at the
same time, and Ol' Mama stands crinkled with age and
thick glasses behind a group of her grandchildren and
their wives. I only know it is her from asking. Her voice
low and coarse, she was not much for small talk. She
drank her share of the whiskey, as likely to pull a pistol
as pull you into her arms.

I can tell you little with absolute certainty except
that if you want to get rich, try drinking. That is to say,
other people's drinking. Snake oil goes down quick in
a cocktail. Harvey Jones had a lesser design, but a design nonetheless, in mind when he took his six sons into
moving moonshine during Prohibition, after the war,
and into the decades of brown-bag laws that kept alcohol out of reach, except if you knew a guy. They were
not alone in the rum-running. Pirates of old favored the
Grand Strand and the Low Country for the same reasons it became popular with the bootleggers, and thus
anyone else looking for a good time. The water, the inlets and marshes and waterways that changed between
storms and by phase of the moon, made hiding out from
the law a breeze. Where Harvey and his sons the Jones
brothers pioneered perhaps was in combining the bootlegging with their other entrepreneurial endeavors, and
putting the money back into Ol' Mama's backroom ca-
sinos. From the postcard, it is easy to see how big the
trunk of a standard car was then. The younger brothers,
my granddaddy among them, kept a whole liquor store

and a cash register hidden in the trunk, selling and dol-
ing change from the parking lots around Myrtle Beach.
So go the family stories passed around like a bottle in
a paper bag. Whenever an unfriendly cop came rolling
by, they simply closed the trunk and drove down the
boulevard.

When the law is not on your side, you pour it a drink
and put it in the hand of a half-naked waitress. The Jones
brothers spent the ensuing decades building more hotels,
buying land and leasing it out, creating the golf courses,
seafood restaurants, and carnivals that bring the tourists
still. It was my great-uncle Keith, the eldest of the six
brothers, who had this vision to go grand, to see high-
rise hotels and resorts decked out in the hedonistic exot-
icism of the Cold War. What goes around comes around,
so they say, and I have wondered if affluence built on
the windfall of vices has some comeuppance brewing
alongside the booze. A rifle propped in the arm of the
couch reaches to be picked up. Touch me. Use me. Hurt
something, and if it's only yourself, then you have done
your heroic best in this life. A bottle of whiskey's not a
Winchester, but few things in this world are portals between the here-on-earth and the gauzy realms of ghosts.
Bullets and bourbon may as well be communion wafers
and the blood of Christ in the swamplands and swashes
of the Low Country.

The Joneses have always felt separated by the lines
of legitimacy and the law from the other contributors to
the community. The two families who separately and as

business partners have owned most of the commercial and residential real estate around Horry County since eighteen hundred and something, the Burroughses and Chapins, rode into town on the railroad, by way of timber. The first railroad between Conway and New Town opened in 1900 and was commissioned so that the Burroughses could move and sell more lumber. The Seaside Inn, the very first hotel in Myrtle Beach, was built when Myrtle Beach was still New Town in 1901 and the Joneses were in Cool Spring.

Before tourism kept us afloat, the longleaf pine forests were sucked dry of the clear, sticky sap to make turpentine and tar for the rest of the world. As far as China, which is about as far as it gets, Carolina tar was famous for its hold. The sap drips still from the longleaf and loblolly pines, sticking to bare feet and fingertips the same as always. A hard scrub with some paint thinner will wash the sap from skin, and nothing but time gets out an indigo stain. Before rice, cotton, or turpentine took off as Low Country staples, enslaved people stirred and beat the soaking indigo plants in brick vats still lined wavy blue in the woods above Charleston to transform this swamp-grown *Indigofera suffruticosa* into blocks of blue mud that dried into gold. For a time in the eighteenth century, during the reign of Queen Anne and during the Golden Age of Piracy, the Long Bay was the world's largest producer of indigo, but not the wild indigo indigenous to the Low Country that grows in sweet stalks of pink flowers that resemble its cousin delphinium, named in Greek for its flowers that bloom in the shape of dolphins. A man known as "Alligator" Stephens published an instructional on getting Bahama indigo from seed to plant to commodity in 1745, but it was Eliza Lucas Pinckney who allowed the Low Country's blood to run blue. The mother of indigo. The mother of patriots. The plantation heiress. Born in Antigua on a British sugarcane plantation before moving to what is now called Bluff Plantation of Wappoo Creek above Charleston, she was sent in 1740 the seeds for Bahama indigo and set about cultivating the hardiest crop and its subsequent production, stealing the methods from the Africans she enslaved. Production slowed only when the colonies declared themselves America, an independent nation, and once the war was won, something called the cotton gin had come to South Carolina. Pinckney is credited by some as the author whose imagination penned the South Carolina agrarian economy and sneered at by others as an overrated archetype, a maternal mascot, who got carried away with the gardening. The names of her sons stain the paper of the Declaration of Independence, and during the Revolutionary War, indigo cakes were the currency of the day. The memory of indigo plantations stains the Low Country as the ink of tattoo parlors bleeds into the landscape today. Land, like the rest of us, must have a hard time letting go, and what's buried is not always treasure. Indigo is the color of the state flag.

Eliza's future husband, a widowed neighbor, once derided her experiments, possible only with the stolen

knowledge and bound hands of enslaved people from
Africa. Their marriage is recollected by history as a
happy one, his opinion of her as a "little visionary" in
one letter might have grown as did her success. If ad-
vancements, even the stolen kind, in the Low Country
must rely on unchaperoned heiresses, it is no wonder
there have been so few. On the subject of pine forests and heiresses, I cannot leave out the legacy of an
Elizabeth Chapin. I never knew a Chapin myself, but
have wished I knew the heiress to the fortune of the
Wall Street mogul Simeon, his daughter Elizabeth. The
Joneses, unlike the Chapins, have never been wealthy
enough to bank on eccentricity, and Elizabeth wore her
nonconforming ideas as fashionably as a mink coat.
She was an avid worshipper of a sect that still makes its
home off of King's Highway, and she built a hideaway
devoted to worshipping the avatar Meher Baba back
in 1944. I stood outside a bar in New York one snowy
night long after I'd moved away and was astounded to
meet a man who had also grown up in Myrtle Beach.
My hometown was not the same as his, however: mine
is a place reputed to have the highest number of strip
clubs per capita in America, with a NASCAR Café and
beach shops that specialize in Confederate flag bikinis,
and this young man had grown up among the untapped
pine trees of Meher Baba's virgin soil. While I cele-
brated my cousin Chris's tenth birthday at the Briarcliffe
Mall Hooters restaurant, this kid was across the street
wrapped in monk's robes and meditating in the middle

of a wildlife sanctuary. Elizabeth's abbreviated story has always floated around town like those long aerial banners advertising happy hour specials and boogie-board rentals that swim across the sky above sunbathers, and I have always envied her the freedom to pay for peace and quiet, and wished it for the women in my story.

While that kind of New Age spirituality might find tolerance on the north end of town, even if hidden in the woods, it wouldn't cut it on the south end, whither we return presently to tally up the Jones men, the sons of Harvey and Ol' Mama. Granddaddy has a picture of all his brothers lined up in middle age along the side of one of their daddy's turquoise Thunderbirds. From left to right in this photograph, the six Jones brothers all wear golf pants in various patterns of checkers and pastels. First we have Keith, who ran the construction company built on moonshine money and who died in a car accident rumored to have been caused by either the mob or the FBI. Then Wilbur, who, before dying of lung cancer at Myrtle Beach Hospital the same summer we expected Granddaddy to die from a mysterious head injury just one floor below, once sued the very same hospital for operating on the wrong leg. Next we have Granddaddy, then Wendell and Herman, and finally Jack. Not pictured is their only sister, Doll, whose real name was Dorothy. As women among men are playthings and novelties, she was only ever called Doll her whole life. I knew Aunt Doll only a little better than I did my great-uncles, half of whom were dead by the time

I came around, but recognized her as another woman raised among men. She kept a neon-green parrot, that we knew as not just mean, but a snitch. It would squawk if my brothers and I ever tried to sneak up her staircase to the forbidden and irresistible second floor, which was every time we were at her house. My second cousin Kay keeps the bird still, and if I were her, I'd have let it fly long ago. In the early 1970s, upon receiving a diagnosis of terminal cancer and dealt two years to live, Harvey hopped in his tomato-red T-bird, picked up his mistress, and drove to Mexico without a word wasted on wife or family. From south of the border, he called Keith, the undoubtedly visionary eldest son, with instructions for the business and no fewer sentimentalities than "Don't fuck anything up." At the end of those two years, when it was clear he was not long for this world, his lady love drove him back up to Ocean View Hospital, which I can't help imagining as the only hospital that matters to us, Myrtle Beach Hospital, and from there, summoned his sons and their sons. These patriarchs with their designs and their dreams of sons. Upon their turn to see their grandfather for the last time, Dad and Les remember sitting in the parking lot, after high school got out but before their shift waiting tables at one of their uncle Herman's seafood joints, smoking Camels, and talking only about what a bastard Harvey had been. Every generation gets a little better, leaves a stitch or two behind to close the open family wounds a little at a time. Their own daddy never up and fled the country for a few years with his mistress, at least. Even considering such a brazen desertion, Ol' Mama did not act too fussed. To notice his leaving would not have brought him back. Women must not only tend to the wound but conceal the scar.

Granddaddy had millions of his own secreted away through investments both known and unknown. He and his brothers had moved up from small-time motels to high-rise hotels and golf courses, had a stake in Holiday Inns from Virginia to Florida. Keith, before he went on the run, from both more hardened criminals than himself and the lawmen after the whole lot, as the family stories go, bought one of the first hotels operating in Myrtle Beach, right next door to the very first. He and his wife turned the Yachts Club into the first high-rise hotel along the Grand Strand, the Yachtsman, which is still there, and while not as nice as it once was, cannot be beat for location, at the mouth of the pier at Fourteenth Avenue North and only a few blocks up from the SkyWheel. The Ferris wheel dreamed up and constructed after I left spins over Ripley's Believe It or Not, which was built during my childhood beside the Pavilion at Ninth Avenue. The Pavilion was the most beloved eleven acres in South Carolina. There bloomed the antiquated rainbow lightbulbs around names of carnival rides spelled out in mosaic mirror tiles. GALAXI and MIND SCRAMBLER twinkled between echoes of roller-coaster laughter and descending screams and the nearby crash of ocean waves for sixty years. The

Pavilion is gone, but Ripley's has recently expanded to include a Haunted Adventure that is open year-round, no longer just at Halloween, and a Maze of Mirrors. The man himself, more popular than President Roosevelt and known as the "biggest liar in the world," drew his fame as a cartoonist for William Randolph Hearst during the Depression. He illustrated oddities he claimed to have seen that were called "fairy tales for grown-ups." Twice a day, tickets are available for tourists to watch bored mermaids with zippered pink tails twirl around an aquarium tank before drying off to catch a shift waiting tables.

My great-uncle Keith might have had a touch of clairvoyance when newly christened Myrtle Beach amounted to a few raised shacks, a handful of hotels, some stray cows and goats ambling on the sand. Does not the very word *inspiration* herald direct and immediate influence from the gods? If such a reach provokes discomfort, then let us call it a prediction. A dream. A bet. A place in time where my imagination meets his. Framed by the dunes, I see his black hair, the same as his brothers', my dad's, my brothers', mine, parted to the side and blown out of place by a breeze that ruffles his tie, nearly the shape and width of a child's kite. As is the style of the time, he wears alligator-skin loafers, and they sink in the fine grains of quartz, smaller and softer underfoot than the hardier sand sucked up from the ocean floor and deposited heavy and rough where the surf breaks. These cool crystals came down from the Appalachian Mountains by natural, elemental means millions of years ago. Even our sand is from someplace else.

"One day," says Keith, recalls my dad, and when I close my eyes, I hear and see it all, too, "this beach will be lined with hotels." And he was right. His legacy now is the Myrtle Beach of spring break and regional family vacations. First hangovers and holes-in-one at Jurassic Mini-Golf. Perhaps not as elegant as the seaside he envisioned, which did exist, however briefly. The luxurious, marble heights of the Ocean Forest Hotel, built in 1930, hosted celebrities from what gets called the Golden Age of Hollywood. It looked like a real castle, not the plaster ones at the theme parks and golf courses around town. Nana once told me she saw Clark Gable on the beach with his pants rolled up to his knees, and I could only bring to mind the image of Drunken Jack the pirate. Like the Pavilion, the historic hotel was torn down for no good reason. The implosion, in 1974, turned the whole town into sightseers for a day.

Hurricane Hazel prompted a construction boom, and Keith began to make good in the hotel business. He and his wife had bought the Yachtsmsan, a club they turned into a high-rise hotel. One local history book hints that its buyers were men of ill repute. Practically ungodly is how it describes the new owners, my relatives, the moonshiners and gamblers. Liking the feel of the hotel business, Uncle Keith, with four of his brothers, bought the Gay Manor Motel from their father, Harvey, and they bought franchising rights to Holiday

Inns between Richmond, Virginia, and Miami, Florida. He was arrested with a ton of marijuana in his car at one point, and according to the rumors, went on the run from the government, drug dealers, the mob, or all three at the end of his life. He just up and disappeared after setting up chains of hotels and motels across the South. Only Uncle Jack knew where they were hiding. Keith sent letters to his mother, Ol' Mama, that Dad found in a shoebox at Nana's house. "Dear Mama," he wrote, "I'm sorry I haven't written. It's been dangerous where I am . . ." Dad and Les remember the FBI coming to their house, led by a Mr. Armstrong, to ask if Granddaddy or the rest of the Jones brothers had any idea where he was hiding. They'd sneak out of bed in their striped pajama sets and press their ears to the walls to listen to G-men ask Herman, Wilbur, Wendell, Jack, and Ralph about their eldest brother, Keith.

My granddaddy claims his crowning achievements as a pair of high-rise hotels, the Sandcastle in central Myrtle Beach, and the Sandcastle South, down toward Garden City. Each is done up as a mauve stucco tower with indoor and outdoor waterslides and a lazy river. The lazy river was always my mom's favorite, and when it seemed like the family was on good terms, or he was out of town, she'd take us to ride its slow circles on sticky yellow inner tubes. I never liked the feeling of being dragged along with only my butt in the water and no say in where I was headed, but she'd close her eyes with one of my baby brothers asleep on her chest and go around and around. It was one of the few times she seemed truly at peace in my childhood. I myself would stand up inside the inner tube and fight the current by walking the other way. When I got to middle school, I refused to get in at all and hid with a book under a tent of damp beach towels.

Granddaddy moved his office to a ground-floor corner of the original Sandcastle and did business with a view of Ocean Boulevard and the National House of Pancakes on the other side of the parking lot. The hotel indeed looked palatial, and countless afternoons when Mom could not chaperone us napping on the lazy river, I led my brothers and cousins, a company of five or six boys, and we skipped across crosswalks at King's Highway, down Ocean Boulevard, past the pier, and crashed the pool. We took turns anointing one another's cheeks with runes in rainbow shades of zinc oxide that doubled as war paint. If ever asked whether we had parents with us or were perhaps hotel guests, we said our grandfather was Ralph Jones, and that was that. If a belt was guaranteed later anyway, we might as well get a few good cannonballs in, and we counted on his employees being as afraid of him as we were.

Though we had free rein at the pool, my parents enjoyed fewer perks of his wealth and spent most afternoons and evenings working at a rotation of pancake houses, seafood buffets, and bars, with the occasional odd job, usually painting houses or doing construction, thrown in as the expenses of living and consecutive children required. Dad's regular daytime gig, before heading out to tend bar or play a show, was managing his uncle Herman's Pancake House in Garden City. My brothers and I spent more time at Nana's house than at our own. Nana glowed surrounded by all of her grandchildren, and she watched us most days while our parents worked. We basked in her supernova-style love, rays of sun without the burn, until we got picked up by our parents or lashed.

Right about when Granddaddy started making plans to buy the Sandcastle, he figured it was high time to move his own family up, if only for appearances. They sold their small house on Thirty-third Avenue across the street from Myrtle Beach High School and next door to the even smaller house of Nana's sister Sue. The neighborhood had been where all the boys went to school and where Nana and Sue every day traded town gossip and snapped beans on their porches with their mother, May Ella, who lived with Sue. Nana and her elder sister Sue were as close as opposite siblings usually are. As olive and dark as Nana was blond and fair, Sue was shy and cautious where Nana was the life of any party, until Granddaddy would notice and threaten her into unnatural smallness. The first night Nana ever spent alone was Sue's wedding night, and they spent a decade as neighbors during the early years of their married lives. One early fall day in 1954, Nana got a call from Mrs. Newton down the street. Her husband worked for the FAA, which had an outpost at the Air Force Base in Myrtle

Beach, and he'd called to warn that the radar indicated
a hurricane had shifted course and was headed straight
for Horry County. By the next morning, the eye was expected right over Myrtle Beach. Mrs. Newton had already sent her two little girls to bang on doors and tell
as many people as they could. Nana and Sue each saddled their babies onto hips and joined the Newtons going door-to-door. Halloween was only two weeks away,
and if they didn't hurry, there might be no need to throw
bedsheets over the kids when it came time to dress up as
ghosts.

You can see the gray gleam of Atlantic ocean from
the end of the street in their old neighborhood, across
King's Highway and at high tide peaking between the
skinny legs of the houses built up on stilts. Other com-
munities went to bed as if it were any other night. Lucky
households woke up to the National Guard banging on
the door at dawn with instructions to leave now with
only the clothes on their backs, and the unlucky woke up
amid the blows of Hurricane Hazel, able only to watch
the mercury in the kitchen barometer sink and sink and
sink and then sink some more. To the lowest level recorded since the Flagg Flood of 1893, which is sometimes
called the Sea Islands Hurricane because the eye passed
over at the Georgia–South Carolina islands, where Gullah is still spoken today, though less and less. Nineteen
fifty-four was only the second year that an official body
started gifting hurricanes with names. Women's names
only, and it would not be until 1979 that the United

States began to name them as men. Fear is a power that runs deep, and if there is anything women are not allowed, it is power. It is as true as it's ever been that what power women have from the toils of tenacity or haphazard luck must be taken away once it is noticed.

After Mrs. Newton's warning, Nana called up Granddaddy at his office at the Sea Dip motel. "Ralph," I can hear her pleading his name over the telephone as I have a thousand times. She'd be sitting, with her legs crossed and her foot rocking her up and down. Picturing her in that little kitchen, I see my uncle Mike on her knee, and know a part of her rocking habit to come from the decades of babies she bounced. I can hear Granddaddy rebuff and ridicule her, as I have heard his voice through the end of the phone all my life. "Please come home, come help. At least meet us at the shelter," she might have said.

He chose to ride out the hurricane with "his people," instead of with his wife and firstborn son. It's not hard for me to conjure the words I've heard him say to her. The hardness in the voice of such a soft woman says it all. It says things like "Jackie, I ain't gonna spend my last moments on earth with you" and "Jackie, you know you're not smart enough to make it up here in time" and "Jackie, why are you doing your best to make me angry . . ."

Nana took shelter not just from high winds and storm surge, but from the contempt of a husband who didn't care to spend with her his last moments on land

and life. With her family, she waited through Hurricane Hazel at the Baptist church downtown with her father, a veteran of World War I who'd been all the way to France and fought at the Battle of the Somme, her sister Sue and her husband and baby. Local history notes that someone took an ax to the wooden planks of the boardwalk underneath the open-air pavilion that had been built in 1949, where the electric carnival would go a decade later. The thinking was that if the rising waters could come up through the floor, the ocean wouldn't push the whole structure down the block, which may have worked. There are reports of similar acts taken in the great Galveston hurricane in Texas fifty years before. The piers and most of the boardwalk along the boulevard broke to pieces and washed away in the storm surge, but the first pavilion was still standing come blue skies.

Hazel is still thought of as the worst hurricane to hit the Carolinas in that century, the twentieth, though the eye veered north, as they usually do, toward the Outer Banks. The eye made landfall near Calabash, North Carolina, barely a game of hopscotch from Little River. Still, the people of the Low Country prayed hard that morning, and, whether it helped or not, only one fatality was recorded in South Carolina. Hundreds of people from Haiti on up to Toronto had gone to God, drowned in the storm surge and flooding rain, under a high tide brought even higher by a full harvest moon that October. The storm surge reached more than twenty feet tall at the high-tide line, and even as the storm lost power moving northward, Hazel managed to fling a gust that remains the strongest wind ever recorded in New York City, 113 miles per hour. Was it during this hurricane, as tornados plucked pines from sandy flat earth and the ocean moved whole city blocks from one side of Ocean Boulevard to the other, as the town congregated by candlelight to pray in creaking pews surrounded by their spouses surely, that Nana first found comfort in words she'd spend the next half a century spelling out in needlepoint and hanging on her walls? *God, grant me the serenity to accept the things I cannot change . . .*

About twenty years ago and forty years on from Hazel, the remaining Jones brothers bought cemetery plots for themselves and their wives. In addition to the one-night stands, they all kept a serious mistress on the side, as their father had, and bought them condos and costume jewelry. There are certain words, like the name of F, with which I do not wish to burden my nana, even in these pages. Mom says she first caught sight of F on the side of Calhoun Road, clearly either on the way to or having left my nana's house. She had a flat tire that I can only rightfully judge as a small act of a god. Nana, who'd spent most of her life suffering blows from Granddaddy, considered his infidelity the most injurious, and like the beatings, just another hurt she had to deal with, a philosophy I found more and more incredulous. What would happen if she let herself get truly angry with him? It was Herman's wife, my great-aunt Frances, who called her up one day and said, "Jackie, you ought to worry about this one. She's a waitress."

If they had gone in together on a mausoleum just for their mistresses, bedecked and bedazzled with busty come-hither angels, it would not have surprised me. Whatever they planned to do with the mistresses, it is unimportant in the scheme of things, as mistresses are. All of the Jones brothers bought husband-and-wife plots—except for Granddaddy, who bought a twin bed of dirt only for himself alongside that of his family and told Nana she could get herself buried down on the south end of Highway 17 next to where her mama and sister lay. It would be Hurricane Hazel all over again. "Even after they're both gone, they won't rest in peace. Jackie's ghost is gonna be walkin' up and down King's Highway lookin' for Ralph, who won't care to see her for eternity," Uncle Leslie has more than once said of his mother's unwavering devotion to a man who hated her more and more for that very thing as the years kept on. She has always simply said to suggestions that she can do better, "He's my husband."

4

Golden Gloves

EARLY ON, WHEN DAD WAS TRYING TO GET MOM to come around to his advances, he called up Nana at the new house on Calhoun Road for some advice. The timber wolf was gone, after all, a promising step toward courtship. "Mama, I wanna send a hundred white roses to this girl I been seeing."

"Well, I reckon you better call up Lazelle's." She directed him to the one-room florist shop, extending the syllables in *Lazelle's* as she coiled the phone cord around a finger tipped in sherbet-peach polish and gazing at the wisteria vines that wrapped around the awning of her patio. Nana told this story from the same rocking recliner in her living room where she would've taken this call decades before. She opened her memory to this chapter as easily as turning to a bookmarked page in one of her library of romance paperbacks that she kept hidden in cupboards and closets around the house. Each of my brothers has had avalanches of bodice rippers fall upon his head when opening forgotten doors. They tumble out of cabinets in cascades of dog-eared longing.

Rocking with one bare foot nestled in the teal shag carpet and the other crossed over her knee, Nana would sway up and down in her rocking chair anticipating the end of her own story. "Son, that many roses is liable to cost a couple hundred dollars." There is coffee percolating in the background and butter beans or cabbage boiling on the stove, which mixes with the moss and roses of perfume. A bouquet of Estée Lauder glass bottles flowers from her bathroom counter. It's in everything, these green and heavy scents, and so much is folded within them too. The carpet's since been pulled up and replaced with cold white tile, but Nana would smile her practiced punch line no matter what was underfoot. Every vowel was a wink when she told stories. "He sent her a dozen white roses instead," she'd say, leaning forward and sliding her bare feet across the carpet or tile, "but I reckon it was enough." Before we were old enough to chase down pirate treasure, Nana was our good fortune and we hers. "When your mama was pregnant with you, I told all my friends, Alverta and Tommy and Ruby Isaac, that I was gonna make my grandchildren love me better than anything. 'Well, how are you gonna do that, Jackie?' they sassed me. I said, 'I'm just gonna love them that way.'

And I did." Children pick up on character as clearly as the weather.

The house on Calhoun Road has always been known to us as "Nana's house," and here I will take what credit is mine, as the first grandkid to use the name that everybody uses just the same as if a painted oar with the words were over the front door like on the vacation homes on Ocean Boulevard. A flick of premonition doled out so innocently by kids, or something said so often it had to come true. Granddaddy sold the little house on Thirty-third Avenue that had weathered Hurricane Hazel and a thousand storms inside. I might venture that he was subliminally drawn, in part, to the street's name. John Calhoun had advocated that South Carolina secede from the Union forty years before the canon fuse was lit at Fort Sumter. Look at any surviving portrait of Calhoun, and see a man burning up with hatred. It's an expression that reminds me of Granddaddy's.

I came to understand, from the first time I saw him raise a hand to Nana, that his inner well of fury ran too deep to be contained in just one body, and that the terrifying anger behind his violence was the spring of his other most defining quality, his racism. We all understood that the targets of his rage were innocent as we were, more innocent most likely, and his hatred of just about everything fueled his words and actions. Kathleen, the maid Nana had hired to keep house when she started keeping books for the family motels, was the only black person allowed inside their house. He spewed hateful language upon catching sight of a person that did not please him, even on the television. Nana warned us with hurricane seriousness never to bring over friends whose very existence would displease him, to save playdates and off-the-cuff invitations to her house for when he was out of town, with his mistress, it was unsaid truth. She thought she was protecting friends and guests, but it was for her sake just as much. To save herself from his fits. Behind his back, sometimes the boys would dare to approach the incantations that scared us more than his belt, to flat out make fun of him because they could. "Granddaddy's two favorite words are damn and the N word," the refrain went. Nothing's funny about the truth in those words, but laughter, like love, is a kind of rebellion. Derision is an easy shield for children trying to protect themselves from hate they don't understand and can't escape. Laughing at him was the only way to gain power over his tyranny.

Nana's house remains the same as during our child-hood, except for the tile that replaced the carpet. It's a sprawling single-story house with a backyard patio that holds up a porch swing and looks onto a tennis court, something called a rock garden that has always just been a circle of small pebbles ringed with monkey grass and camellia trees, a concrete pool set into the top of a small slope that leads to the one-bedroom Back House and a gardener's shed. All of this is crowned on the far end by the great magnolia tree, which is without question the best kind of tree for climbing. I have never seen the pool, outfitted with a rusted, crumbling plaster diving board, with any water but a foot of slimy green pond scum that houses families of giant toads and patches of cattail reeds.

The pool was filled with clean swimming water for only their first year on Calhoun Road. Not long after the furniture was moved in and bags were unpacked, Granddaddy and Nana flew to Las Vegas, where the Jones brothers and their wives—and on other trips, their mistresses—went to golf and rub shoulders with gangsters and wannabes like themselves. They left Dad and Leslie in the care of Kathleen, who had worked for the family since the days of the Sea Dip, when she drove up from Georgetown in an old pickup truck whose bed was filled with other black women who commuted to Myrtle Beach to clean the motels that appeared along Ocean Boulevard. When my parents could not afford to buy a crib for me, it was Kathleen who gifted them one of polished walnut. Had she wanted to cool her feet in the water of the pretty seascape held in the windows of the motel rooms she cleaned, she would not have been allowed. Black vacationers were banned from the beaches, as well as motels and hotels and restaurants, and had to venture half an hour north to Atlantic Beach to enjoy the water. Until the mid-1960s, ropes were strung across the beach and well past the breaking waves at the borders of Atlantic Beach to keep sand and sea segregated.

Mike threw a pool party in his parents' absence, and most of Myrtle Beach High School played quarters on the patio in between make-out sessions in the pool and god knows what else in the Back House. Kathleen, her everyday kindness steeled into the practicalities of survival when faced with a yard full of drunk and coked-up white teenagers, locked herself and the two younger boys in a bedroom and called the police. After that, Granddaddy drained the pool. He had an excuse to throw a few punches at Mike, not that he ever needed any, and to then throw him out of the house for good. He had already kicked him out once for refusing to crop his hair military-short, probably hoping that he'd be drafted sooner rather than later. Such was the offense of needing your bangs trimmed, were you male. At fourteen, Dad brought home a friend who Granddaddy chased out of the house with fists raised for daring to have his hair down to his shoulders. This the son of one of Nana's best friends. When Dad went outside to apologize, his friend handed him *Honky Chateau*, the new Elton John album that had just come out. "No hard feelings, man," he said as he passed to my dad the album that he played the most in high school. In the same bedroom Kathleen had once locked them inside, he had found the record that inspired him to learn how to write his own songs, grow a beard, and stop cutting his own hair.

Uncle Mike, as the firstborn, took a lot of the hits. What drives a man to hate his own son from the very beginning? Nana often said she thought he was jealous. Mike had been conceived after an impatient engagement that lasted just a few hours. They were married at the courthouse and spent their wedding night in Nana's office at the local bank, South Carolina National, where she was a bank teller and a bookkeeper. She had some numbers to finish before they could enjoy any celebrations. Now maybe it is perhaps more apparent why Nana's mom, May Ella, thought of him more as a horse thief than a son-in-law. Mike was born while Granddaddy was stationed in San Diego with the Navy, where he discovered not a love of the sea, but a talent for boxing. He even won the Golden Gloves competition in the flyweight division. A local newspaper described him as "scrappy." I have never seen Granddaddy on the beach, despite his milking its charms for his bottom line. He may be the only person in Myrtle Beach who never bothers to consult with the ocean. When he came home, he put all of his energy into throwing punches at his family. "Come look at these photographs of your granddaddy," Nana has begged often. A scrapbook of his boxing days sits where it always has on a shelf of photo albums. She seems proud of him, and I wonder if that is her defense of what she knows we have seen. "If it is enough for me to put up with, then can't nobody say it's too much," she may as well have said.

There is no denying that Mike has alternatively been called both a fuckup and a genius. When his number came up during Vietnam, as Granddaddy hoped it would, I am sure, he didn't pass the physical. He had been born deaf in one ear, the Army doctor said, and he danced up and down the bus on the way back to town from the base. "Your number got called up?" he asked the grim-faced teenage boys in their new uniforms returning to Myrtle Beach on the bus from Conway. "Why don't you give me your girlfriend's number since I'm gonna be staying here," he'd recount to me and the boys before we knew what Vietnam was. He was the first of the brothers to divorce, still a semi-scandal back in 1990 South Carolina. Though Mike's two sons would have been better off with their mother, Granddaddy is said to have had words with the judge seeing to custody matters. Mike got both boys full-time. What backwoods Southern judge didn't regard tribal masculinity as justice of the first order? Granddaddy didn't care a lick about my cousins, Chris and Brian, but they were property like any other that he knew how to take. Fairness, like compassion, belongs to the fantasies of women. Mike moved into the Back House, and Chris and Brian moved into Nana's house, where, in front of the rest of us, Granddaddy let loose on my two little cousins for no reason other than they were Mike's. The only salve for this renewed generational trauma was the tender attentions of Nana.

Often when the boys and I were at Nana's, Mike offered us each a few bucks to clean the Back House for him. This usually meant that he was expecting a date. He'd herd us all into the one-bedroom house beside the carport, promise us a dollar or two, and leave again in a disheveled frenzy. I was seven when he moved in back there, so my brothers and cousins were a year to a few years younger, and we were all young enough to feel like we had to do what he told us to do, while also knowing fully that Mike, as he had no authority over anything, really had none over us. We made a show of tidying up at first, and once alone, covered the walls and refrigerators with stickers and drawings. We went through his drawers and shelves, of course, pocketing any cash or coins that we knew from experience he'd never pay us after promising a going rate. Inevitably one of us would come across assorted tablets and bags of powder in between couch cushions and next to ashtrays, and we knew somehow that it was what was called "drugs," without quite grasping exactly what that was.

I was living in a northern city after college, working at a bookstore and tinkering for the first time with writing my own stories, still fantasies about living abroad, of Sardinian summers and wine-dark seas, or monastic peace on Himalayan mountaintops, when I was summoned to Myrtle Beach. Mike had had a stroke. In fact, he'd had several and was laid up at Myrtle Beach Hospital, unable to move or speak. By that time, he lived alone on the inland side of the Waterway on the way to Socastee. After the first stroke, he'd fallen between his bed and a wall, unable to get up or call for help. Nobody found him for days, and Mike had another series of strokes. Leslie and a cousin found him, after Nana called up both of them saying, "I want y'all to go check on Mike." It was unusual that he would go so long without asking her for money or favors.

After Granddaddy joined the rest of the family at Nana's house, the doctor called him up with an update on the condition of his eldest son. I watched him go from his typical "Howdy, howdy" on the phone with a fellow member of the Horry County Boys' Club to fuming in the space of a breath. Mike's blood-test results showed an array of unnatural substances in the blood. His strokes were no longer a temptation to pity the bad luck of his firstborn, but cause to double down on his bitter hatred. Granddaddy, always so angry and ashamed of his son, couldn't contain his wrath, but with a glance at me adjusted his anger. I had assumed he had wanted to spare my ladylike sensibilities, which would surely be shocked to hear the word *cocaine*, as if I had not been picking up little plastic bags of it in the Back House since the second grade. Now I think it was his own embarrassment he sought to hide. "It's that goddamn," he began to shout and looked at me, "that goddamn Coca-Cola. Michael hadn't got one bit of sense messing around with that goddamn Coca-Cola." Mike got his speech back, slow and slurred, and returned to the Back House in a wheelchair.

Chris must have been only thirteen when he was kicked out of the only place he'd really ever called home, however unwelcoming half the household had been. Nana took Chris and his younger brother, Brian, to school, fed them, checked their homework, and made sure their favorite cookies were kept in the house, generally acting as maternal as possible after their own mother was swindled out of custody. Nana was the only stable, loving presence for them there, and as one of the many ways Granddaddy would belittle her daily in our collective presence, he made a show of telling my cousins how worthless they were. "They won't amount to nothin', Jackie, why waste your time and my money on them?" he asked, even though it was his machinations that brought them into his house. He never bothered to hide his hatred for whatever he decided deserved his ire, and as extensions of the son he hated, Chris and Brian were easy targets. The gist of the refrain changed little, except occasionally that he raised a hand to her or one of us, or called her names. And yet we had all grown so used to this; the heaviness of my memory of this particular incident is my own teenage sadness at being by then only a visitor for these scenes and knowing that I'd never know the true extent of their torture. We'd just moved away, to Charlotte, and so my brothers and I were visitors ourselves.

Granddaddy's violence needed no provocation. At thirteen, Chris was a young man in need of recognition and a child in need of attention. He was smart and caring enough to take the heat off his grandmother, who defended him daily at her own expense. On this evening in my memory, I sat at the kitchen table in front of her coffee maker and next to the decorative stained-glass hands in prayer. Whose hands were they, I still wonder. Jesus's? Suddenly, Chris and Granddaddy were screaming at each other in the doorway between the living room and the long, dark hallway. It's a scene that I can rewind to watch over and over, and though it is mercifully muted, I would prefer to reclaim the space and forget it altogether. I can feel the distress of my nana, which burns my skin worse than a sunburn. She moves to intervene and then stops. Chris was a star player on the school baseball team then, and Granddaddy picked up his baseball bat. The moment of wondering if he will actually use it lasts as long as the rest of the memory. Chris took off running down the hallway, and we all jumped up and ran after them. Having reached the end of the hallway, Chris turned around. Something in him changed or else he had nowhere to go. He reached out and took the bat from Granddaddy's hand. Here again history has repeated itself as unfailingly as a chorus. Granddaddy had been in nearly the same position before, nearly in that exact spot some twenty years before, when his two younger teenage sons, Dad and Les, caught his arms on their way down to Nana's back and told him, "Never again." At least, not in front of them.

If I were a scientist or a believer, I might posit the existence of a black hole at the end of that hallway. Nothing so fancy as time travel or teleportation, but it was as if I were watching both scenes play out at once and caught a flicker of intergenerational déjà vu across my cousin's face that gave him the strength to say, "Never again." My mind is not so superstitious as some, but there are indisputable events that appear before you plain as day, no matter how much you wish they wouldn't. Granddaddy shoved him aside and locked himself in his bed-room, and Chris stalked the hallway, smashing the glass in every family picture and the embroidered "Serenity Prayer," leaving a trail of blood and broken glass but taking the baseball bat with him and leaving the house for good.

Granddaddy forbade Chris entry to the house, and though Nana would sneak him in and offer him what-ever she could, the fear of being discovered kept their visits short and fraught. His moment of casting off his bruised childhood was surely as freeing as it was terri-fying, but it also bound Chris even closer to his captor. That spark of rage that festered into hatred was now given free rein to rot away at his own insides. He went to live with Uncle Les and Ralph Howard for a time. He lived with his mother on and off, and between corners and shelters. Nobody knew it until it was too late, but he was already buying his own white powders, first the same crushed-up pills and cocaine his father preferred, and then heroin. What else but opium to dull both pain and hatred, while giving yourself more of each with ev-ery hit.

I once described Nana and Granddaddy, when asked by a boyfriend's parents about my family history, as "high school sweethearts." I was caught off-guard, and they had indeed gone to school together, meeting for dates at the Pavilion and the boardwalk, dancing the shag on Ocean Boulevard as kids. More out of panic than deceit, I wanted to be liked and welcomed into a family whose uncomplicated affection I wanted to know better. "Yeah, real sweet," said the guy I was going out with, whom I'd met at our fancy New York college. He gave me the same disbelieving face of a friend who'd gone to Harvard, whose ancestors were Ivy League–educated back to the *Mayflower*, when I mentioned that one of my brothers had dropped out of high school. Like I'd just revealed that I had met a Martian, though I guess that was her feeling. I could distance myself from my Southern ghosts, from the lowness I felt I was from for so long, but I feared that I would never belong or be understood anywhere else. I mistook these moments of cultural dissonance as signs that my fears were truths and removed myself a little at a time from where I worked hard to get and then wondered why I felt so distant from both who I was born as and who I wanted to be.

A neat and tidy cycle that I could not talk about with anyone except my other grandfather, Henry. I used to think I had a good grandfather and a bad grandfather. In any case, Grandpa Henry knew the feeling of living among outsiders, the educated a few rungs up the ladder of class, and sticking out even though you want not to be noticed at all, even when being noticed for something is part of what got you ahead in the first place. Aspiration is somehow lauded and clawed at. "Just smile and be yourself, kid," he'd sooth, when I'd tell him how I felt. "Grandpa, but I feel like I don't belong," I'd go on, meaning first to the hallowed halls of my university—but it's not time for the relief of his faith in me just yet.

Soon enough we'll be sipping on whiskey and ginger ale and sharing stories with him under the scuppernong vine. We are still in Myrtle Beach at the moment, and he is a four-hour drive away.

Why on earth did Nana marry Granddaddy? When did he go from a shy kid taking his girl on spins around the old Ferris wheel to chasing his grandchildren down a hallway with a baseball bat? His own father, that old moonshiner Harvey, was said to knock his boys around. Did Granddaddy catch or inherit from his father what he got beaten into him? Nearness to violence taints our imaginations, the images we acquire must have some power to influence our bodies to action, and it is the hardest of things to stop imagining the worst once your mind's in motion. At a certain point, there is the choice to use this chain to hurt instead of breaking it. "Look at this," Dad once said to me, as he passed his phone from his rocking chair to mine on a front porch many years into the future from my memory of that day at Nana's house. He had a video going, of a friend of his, singing a song called "Hurt People Hurt People," and I could see the hairs on Dad's forearm standing up straight at the simplest of lines.

Everyone she was related to, which is a lot of folks, and a few she wasn't, told Nana to leave him. "He's my husband," she said as she always and only ever said. Nana was no gold digger, but she was both too smart and too pretty not to be aware of the value of her beauty as a useful asset. The Joneses had their money by then, and were known for being a little dangerous. The thrill of danger gets awfully mixed up with the butterflies of love, though I have no doubt she loved him no matter how much he hurt her. I can feel the cool white tile of her living room underfoot as I imagine her telling the story of how her grandfather on the Hardee side was swindled out of their family land near Galivants Ferry, where the alligator- and cottonmouth-filled swamps that flank the Little Pee Dee River dry out into fields of tobacco farmland loomed over by crumbling plantations. As told to her by her parents and she tells it, too. A neighbor figured he might expand his acreage by accusing my great-great-grandfather of sleeping with his wife. That way, this neighbor could shoot dead my great-great-grandfather and buy off both judge and jury. Then he would be free to kick the grieving widow off her land. So the story goes.

I took the liberty, however, as she must have done, too, of interpreting this tale as a reminder that resources included husbands. A husband would have been the most valuable resource. As she'd say freely, perhaps in contrast with me, she "developed early," and was a Hitchcock blonde by age fourteen at a time when there was nothing better a woman could be. Even if she'd gone on to get her college degree, she was first and foremost a creature built to love who wanted to be loved in return. In a land ruled by men, an open book is not as safe and half as warm as open arms. As she built a small kingdom out of her children's and grandchildren's adoration, perhaps the skin of reality stretched thinner and thinner, so that a realm owned by women built between letters and pages could be penned with growing ease to temper the harsher dimensions of her married life.

More important, she was in love, as she said. She had won a scholarship to Winthrop College, an all-girls school upstate in the red-dirt piedmont that she attended for a semester. Her mother and sister sewed her a single skirt and blazer, as they were too poor to buy any of the required uniform. After her first semester, her own daddy had a heart attack, and she gave up on college to go to work as a bank teller to support her ailing parents. Someplace in the world there is a language wherein the word for man translates the same as the word for burden.

Nana kept on her coffee table next to the photo albums a book of folktales and ghost stories from the Low Country. The author, a woman, I remember noticing, claimed on the inside that a librarian at the Library of Congress told her that South Carolina is the state with the most folktales in the whole of the U.S. Nonetheless, it was a thin volume with its title in white letters over a photo of live oaks and their Spanish moss in which I found the tale of Alice Flagg, a ghost story I'd heard from Dad and Uncle Leslie many times by candlelight on stormy evenings and before their dinner shifts at whatever seafood joint they were working at the time. Finding this well-known oral story printed on paper served to amplify the power of all the other oral history I'd heard in passing. It seemed to mean that everything I'd heard was true. You will kindly forgive my retelling if you have heard this story already.

Dr. Allard Flagg was a young and respectable Low Country physician, and he and his mama and sister, Alice, lived in a white plantation house known as the Hermitage. I went to visit the place as a girl, and maybe I forgot to hold my breath going past the family graves, as I have carried Alice's story with me. Her grave, a flat slab of marble on the ground, is marked only with AL-ICE. Alice fell in love, as pretty young girls are supposed to do, but her brother found the object of her adoration, a turpentine salesman, unacceptable. Dr. Flagg sent Alice off to boarding school in Charleston, where she took down with something called "country fever," which the dictionary will tell you is an old-timey term for malaria. She was shipped back to the Hermitage, where Dr. Flagg, in treating her, discovered a ring on a yellow ribbon that she had tied around her neck. While Alice was hallucinating with fever and heartbreak, her loving brother took her engagement ring and threw it into the swamp. Naturally Alice died of malaria, or to spite her brother as I would interpret, though heartbreak is the scientific cause of death usually given in the stories. She's spent the last two hundred years walking the gardens of the Hermitage looking for her ring. I guess jewelry lasts longer than romance in the afterlife, too. Rereading the story as a girl from Nana's recliner, my mind of its own accord saw Granddaddy as the controlling, vindictive doctor, and Nana as the lovesick belle who walks the earth looking for, if not her lover, the evidence that she was loved.

5

Waccamaw Academy

I ASKED NANA WOULDN'T SHE LIKE TO FINISH up college, get her degree. Ever the Southern lady, she only said how proud she was of me. Was it the decades of hearing Granddaddy say "Jackie ain't got the sense" or "Jackie, nobody wants to hear what you have to say" to strangers and family? The shameful sigh of relief in realizing that insults were all for now. A half century of diminishment where there should have been affection takes a toll on the most tenacious of spirit, and to hear her describe herself as Granddaddy would upon breaking a nail or misplacing a phone number brought out, well, speak of the devil. It brought out Granddaddy's temper in me. "I wish you wouldn't call yourself stupid-fatugly," I'd say. I found myself angry with her putting up with his abuses, but I was mad at myself for feeling his anger come out in me. An unfair and even crueler response than the words of a small, petty man.

My mom and Nana enrolled me, and my brothers too, lest we forget them, in a small private school in Horry County. Mom begged the tuition from her father back in Charlotte, a small humiliation that would change my life. My parents' income came mostly from waiting tables, and they had put all their savings toward buying a little brown house in Conway. In a small wonder in the biggest county east of the Mississippi, Waccamaw Academy was only a short drive from our little brown house in Conway. I did not realize how big this tiny house was in my memory until the last time I left Myrtle Beach, when I took a detour to drive by the old neighborhood on the way out of town. I could practically see my dad and Jack in his white Cadillac, see the steamboat straight out of Mark Twain that had been docked there throughout my childhood. Is it that the recollection of life from a child's wide eyes and narrow world feels bigger, or that we were looking down from the peak of our happiness? I was shocked to see our little brown house barely bigger than a double-wide trailer, though still surrounded on two sides by pine forest and kudzu vines, and on the third by blackberry brambles, where a family of black snakes used to live. I recall here a line from Amy Hempel that I cling to as my nana would a proverb. "What seems dangerous often is not—black snakes, for example, or clear-air turbulence." Of black snakes, Dad always said, "They're the good guys." The only good guys in our story, though take care in their company, as even a venomless bite can scar.

As children at the little brown house, we spent our days digging holes for no reason at all. We wrestled and fought until Bandit, our collie with a strip of orange across his eyes, pulled us off one another by the neck of our T-shirts. Dad had taught the collie to intervene when it looked as if somebody was getting hurt. We hunted lizards of glow-in-the-dark green on the ringing chain-link fence that surrounded our backyard. Once captured in little palms for cups, we coaxed open their mouths with delicate strokes on their bubbling red throats and let them snap shut on our earlobes and dangle like earrings. We dug holes in the backyard looking for pirate treasure and when none was found, I would become the pirate and offer treasure from the house to be buried. One of the few things Nana ever got mad at me for was burying a bumblebee-shaped broach she had given me made from stripes of black enamel and real gold, its wings twinkling diamonds. She and Mom took their turn as treasure hunters and shoveled up the whole backyard looking for it. Still there like the corn snake lost in the house. There was always the family of snakes who lived under the shed and were good for sport. Dad once found us out there using a stick to flip one of these serpents, banded in candy-corn colors, into the air like it was a pancake, and moving quick as an adder himself, ran in quick strides to knock the stick out of my

brother Justin's hand and pull us away. I can still see the
stripes pinwheeling through the air, scarlet and saffron
spinning brightly against a cornflower blue sky, before it
tumbled down to a dusty and stunned landing. "What
in the hell?" So unfurled the litany. "Don't y'all know
any better than to be poking at a poisonous snake?"

He got a good look, once it hit the ground, mutter-
ing under his breath counting snakeskin rings with an
outstretched finger. "Red on black, friend of Jack. Red
on yellow, kill a fellow." It was a king snake and not the
near-identical coral snake, whose bite is the closest thing
on this continent to a cobra's. They are thought of, coral
snakes, as docile and slow compared with the muscle of
a cottonmouth or the meanness of a copperhead.

"Leave the poor guy alone. He's just a tired old
kingsnake, probably got a family to take care of under
there. Go on little guy, go on," Dad said in a gentle tone
for the poor animal. Perhaps he was thinking of the time
he was scolded as a child for playing with toy soldiers.
He'd knotted shoelaces around the plastic necks of a few
traitors and flung them over a chair, only to have May
Ella, Grandmama as he called her, scream and run out of
the room. Nana took her youngest boy against her side
and explained that as a girl, her mother had seen a man
hanged from a tree by a mob. We nested under Dad's
arms and squatted down to watch our friend slither
home. It was a game we kept on playing even after this
scene, and when that king snake decided it was time to
wriggle up the social ladder and move on up to a better

neighborhood, Justin took to throwing the cat up in the air, which seemed to bother nobody, not even the cat, a brave ginger tabby we called Toffee, who developed gangrene after someone shot a BB pellet into his thigh.

When we were old enough, my brothers and I were enrolled in school at Waccamaw Academy, named for the indigenous people who built their villages among the loblolly pines in the gum-cypress wetlands and blackwater swamps spilling between the banks of what is now the Waccamaw River and the Pee Dee River and who almost certainly did not wear the feathered and tasseled crown of the school's sports uniforms, printed in indigo blue on cotton sweatshirts. Before the first Roanoke colony was established and then unaccountably disappeared in North Carolina, before Jamestown was settled and heralded as the New World in Virginia, and a century before the *Mayflower* landed at Plymouth Rock, a Spanish colony was attempted in 1526, near present-day Georgetown, an hour south of Waccamaw Academy, by the Spaniard Lucas Vázquez de Ayllón, an acquaintance of Diego Columbus, son of Christopher. Ayllón, the forgotten conquistador of the Carolinas. He called his settlement San Miguel de Gualdape, after sailing a Spanish caravel from Hispaniola to claim the boggy pluff mud for the Spanish crown. Did it seem a cursed mission, a cursed place from the beginning? The flagship, *Capitana*, struck a sandbar and sank, and the group's supplies were lost. The shipwreck is thought to rest underneath North Island near Georgetown, the land itself moved by centuries of storms and shifts to hide the ship from scholars and treasure hunters alike. San Miguel de Gualdape is recognized by historians as the very first European settlement in the United States. The first place in the United States where enslaved people from Africa were brought ashore, too. And the site of the first revolt of enslaved people in the United States. Only a few months into his venture, Ayllón died of some illness, perhaps the country fever that took Alice Flagg, or the smallpox or measles he passed to the Waccamaw, which would kill nearly the whole population and erase their language forever. The few European survivors abandoned South Carolina soon after, until the English came a hundred years later.

For a while, I searched for the translations of any journals or letters he might have left behind. I have had to settle for secondhand accounts and the journals of Cabeza de Vaca, the Spanish soldier shipwrecked near Galveston, Texas, in 1528, after a hurricane claimed his ship. Left for dead, like Drunken Jack, but washed ashore with more faith than rum. He and the few survivors walked for eight years, from the Island of Doom, the name they gave to Galveston, until they found a Spanish outpost in Mexico. The slim purple edition of this account was published as part of a series on explorers that included an abridged account of the travels of Marco Polo, who claimed therein to have seen a griffin, the mystical lion-eagle hybrid, in flight somewhere near what is now Zanzibar or Madagascar.

So close to the river was Waccamaw Academy that when the banks overflowed from rain, storm, or tides, the football field returned to swamp. Practices and field days had to be adjusted when the presence of alligators on the grass deterred the presence of small student bodies. The yellow speckled necks of snapping turtles were given a reprieve by so many carpooling mothers that a permanent ban was issued declaring NO VACANCY in the classroom aquariums. At the risk of provoking tempers unknown, I advise travelers to leave them be on the side of the road, or to push them into a ditch with the longest nearby stick. They've been known to bite off fingertips, and I have watched one of these little dinosaurs eat a fuzzy duckling whole. The sea turtles of our fair coast, on the other hand, emerge gentle and lovely from the cool cover of quartzy moonlit sand to be lapped up by the high tide. As such, they are state-protected tourist attractions, bumper-sticker symbols of pride, and interference earns a hefty fine or jail time.

I spent at least one afternoon a week on the reptile-friendly football field not for love of sport or school spirit, but because bomb threats were called in regularly by bored or ill-prepared students. I have a memory of poking with the end of a fallen brown pine needle the pink wide-open mouth of a Venus flytrap while I waited to be led back to class. Stalking patches of brighter green in the soft soggy grass. The sticky shine of its body unhinged to a summery pink that recalled the sweetness of watermelon and the scent of powdered cubes of bubble gum. And then the surrounding fringe of teeth sharp and thin to cage its meals, or in the case of my memory, closing calm and slow around the tip of pine needles. Here is probably my chance to note that this carnivorous plant, a strange hybrid rare and beautiful, grows only in the swamplands that bridge the border of the Carolinas. If the observations of Ayllón were published in a slim edition alongside those of more famous explorers, would these plants appear as monsters or wonders? Would he have exaggerated their size so that grown men were seen eaten alive by swamp monsters in pages presented to European kings? Looking at its insides so freely offered, I thought then that it looked not monstrous, but like a valentine cut out from stiff construction paper.

Waiting for the police or fire department to declare the school safe, the whole school stood and looked out into the pine and cypress at the edges of the field. Floating between the tiers of tree limbs, glowing lights are commonly observed in these swamps. Swamp gas and fox fire are the explanations. Those for whom bioluminescence is not magical enough claim one ghost story or another, depending on what suits them. There are the Bingham Lights in Dillon. The Land's End Lights in Beaufort. Lights of the Old Hanging Tree, from which the eyes of murdered enslaved people do not sleep. Headless soldiers in uniforms blue and gray hold lights aloft, looking for their lost heads. A region in search of reasons for the violence of its past, not ready to give up its ghosts and the guilt that brings them ever back to life. The only orbs of light I can report seeing are the Fourth of July fireworks shot up from the community college next to the Witch Links golf course in Conway. Dad would pile us into the bed of his pickup truck, the one Uncle Jack ran off the road and the one Hank Williams Jr. sings about, with folding beach chairs of woven plastic strips and rusty legs. Our family watched the fireworks pop and sizzle, under the sulfurous spell of gunpowder and a bucket of fried chicken picked up along the way. "Y'all, pile in," Dad said, directing us to jump into the back of the truck with the dog and ride with him down to the bait shop to get cigarettes and candy. On the way back home, I'd rest my chin on the edge of the truck next to Bandit's, and the wind blew his long, muddy hair into mine. Dad and Leslie managed to find houses just down the street from each other, like Nana and Sue thirty years before them, and the boys and I played with Leslie's son, Ralph Howard, as another brother. Mom baked pies from blackberries we picked with purple-stained fingertips, our toes as far away from the snaky bramble as possible, as Dad wrote love songs from the couch or a makeshift desk in the garage where the King took it all in. On a bitter cold night many years later, at a bar in New York, Dad confessed that those were the happiest days of his life, and I must concur that it was an idyllic time until it wasn't.

The longest I've ever lived in one place is still that little, love-filled house in Conway. The spot where we watched fireworks every July is now a fully developed suburb of strip malls, home to vape shops and tattoo

parlors and revolving-door apartment complexes of the
newly divorced and the new to town. Conway is, like
Little River to the north, one of the older outposts in
Horry County and far more historical than the newer
Myrtle Beach, which was called New Town until 1900,
when a contest was held among the county's turpentine
laborers and socialites. The wife of the nearest railroad
baron, one Mrs. Burroughs, suggested the winning pick.
Imagine that. The wax myrtle bushes that fringed the
beach's dunes are rarer now, pulled up for hotel development. I thought for a while as a kid that the whole town
was named for the crape myrtle trees in my nana's backyard. They flowered always, no matter the season, which
I know is not their usual pattern, but I must ask for your
trust when I say that on any day of the year, when you
creaked open the wooden door painted a glossy, chip-
ping beige, swishes of hot pink twirled at your ears and
danced at your heels to lie finally underfoot as you followed the last visitor's trail of flattened petals to the patio door, where Nana sat rocking in her chair waiting
for company. She was the center of our universe then,
so why wouldn't she be that of the whole town? Upon
finding for the first time Florence, Italy, on a map, I de-
duced in the logic of nursery school solipsism that the
town was named for the Florence, South Carolina, we
drove through on the way to Grandpa's house. Myrtle
Beach has remained true to the spirit of its founding as a
town that favors both nepotism and contests, the latter
of which are more bikini-oriented these days.

It was at Waccamaw Academy I met my first friend, a round-faced girl named Dora who liked to eat handfuls of dog kibble and whose mother advised matriculation into the circuit of pageants that fostered all the little girls of future means, including Dora. Just like my dad had a string of bars to perform at, so the girl children of the county had stages erected to show off their bodies in malls both shopping and strip. In a culture that valued more highly its barriers than the diligent or lucky few who managed to scramble over them, it must have seemed like an opportunity for advancement. Mom's father had never owned a pair of shoes until enlisting in the Air Force, and she and her sisters relied on the generosity of an aunt to sew their church clothes for most of their childhood. Just a generation between naked poverty and literal pageantry. We want things to be easy for those we love, to spare them pain, of course, and to spare ourselves the suffering by proxy. Pink. The color I knew as winking Venus flytraps. Bubble gum in squares. Calamine lotion for sunburn and chicken pox. A color I would learn to hate as I was pinned and sashed into its various shades for the length of my time at Waccamaw Academy. I would be socializing with the children of the oldest and richest families in Horry County, whose great-grandparents had named the town and built the railroad that replaced the ferry that had been carting day-trippers across the Pee Dee River to New Town.

Nana had grown up in the shadow of Miss Sun Fun pageants, watching girls less lovely than she wave in their swimsuits from parade floats every year as she worked double-time at the bank and at Myrtle Beach High School. For both Nana and Mom, for whatever else they endured, being considered beautiful by men made the world a little less hard for them. I had inherited none of their looks, resembling neither of these women who put stock in their most valuable commodity, as it was shown to them. Nana used to say, "If you marry a Jones, all your children come out looking like Joneses," which is what I looked like.

Dora was an only child, and her house felt like an enchanted hideaway to me, a different reality built inside a stilt-raised beach house that was secluded instead among swamp forests and live oaks draped with moss and cottonmouths next to the Waccamaw River. Before we were allowed to go downstairs and play on their lawn, which overlooked the river, her father made us wait inside while he and his shotgun patrolled the area for water moccasins that slithered up from the river and dropped from the treetops onto the grass. Like the upper classes everywhere, Dora's family liked to hunt, and pictures of her grinning beside her father in matching fatigues with an assortment of newly dead creatures, fish, quail, ducks hanging from the mouths of their hunting dogs, did not suggest to me the actions required to get to that point of posing. These photographs decorated the walls of their home, accenting the stuffed and tastefully shellacked mallards posed forever in midflight above the fireplace. Their violence was a controlled one that could be mounted and shown off. Our violence was never spoken of. A shameful secret. Only once was I strapped on the back of a four-wheeler and forced to accompany their party as they shot the deer I loved to spot between the pines on the side of the road.

Occasionally after school, Dora's mother, Miss Dorothy, would take us out for afternoon drinks, as it were, an event that expected a certain level of decorum. I politely crossed my ankles and kept my elbows off the table, as she'd instructed once before. Miss Dorothy ordered a round of Shirley Temples for the three of us. "Stick your chest out, girls," she corrected our posture continually and in any location, restaurant booths, school parking lot, their kitchen, or on pageant stage, and it irked me even then to be coached to put first and foremost the fated legal tender of my gender's strongest currency. Still, every time I lugged myself into the back seat of her sports utility vehicle, I hoped we would end up at the dark restaurant with the black leather booths and fizzy pink drinks with prim red cherries on top. It was a luxury, their manners somewhat exotic at first introduction. I had been to bars before or after shifts with my parents, played with peanut shells discarded on the floor as Dad sang onstage, but we could not afford sit-down restaurants then, though the Joneses owned quite a few. It was a treat when Dad and I slid into his pickup truck to go get biscuits from the drive-through place called Oliver's. Such was the contrast of my early childhood: we were barely able to pay for groceries, and yet

I received fur coats and collectible dolls as Christmas gifts from Nana and Granddaddy. It was just the way I knew things. I dreaded Christmases, knowing that for gifts I'd receive elaborate costumes of my own that I would then be forced to parade. Like the pink suede cowgirl skirt and vest, complete with fringe and boots. And the white rabbit-fur coat and matching muff, as if I were Natasha Rostov. Nana only gave me what she must have dreamed of herself as a girl, and I was luckier than Chris and Brian, for whom Granddaddy cussed at the thought of buying milk for their cereal. That there was family money floating around out there somewhere just out of reach was like a life raft in the deep end of a pool, and that helped us sleep most nights. Riches that were out of place among the spare treats my parents afforded for us, after months of layaway at Brendle's and Roses. At birthdays and Christmases, Nana gave Mom money and directed her as to what to buy for her, so that her pride would not suffer at having no gifts to give. Palm-size compacts in enameled and bejeweled shapes hid waxy Estée Lauder scents. Leopards and carousels like the one at the Pavilion, sea turtles and seashells, and butterflies and cabochons remind me always of White Diamonds and White Linen. If she smelled like Elizabeth Taylor, she could be more like her in other ways. "You know," Nana would say of Taylor, "she's had eight husbands."

Comparing, comparing, always I was comparing. A pedagogical device picked up from homework, coloring

books, magazines for children. Spot the differences in
these pictures, these stories, these bodies, these lives.
The feeling that I was out of place continued to grow the
more I compared. I was a quiet and responsible child,
but bossy and bookish enough to inflict concern. It was
me and not a brother or cousin who led our way down
the line of hotels on Ocean Boulevard, in and out of
pools at the oceanfront hotels. Yet I was the only one
told to cross my legs or sit quiet, but also stick out my
chest somehow. To put down my homework and help fix
supper. "You're the most responsible," Mom said as a
compliment when I complained that I'd rather be participating in pine-cone throwing or freeze tag. An assess-
ment of truth, but only because responsibility was foisted
upon my little suntanned shoulders. Responsibility was
never, ever expected from the boys, most only a year or
two younger. A different shade of anger, the silent re-
sentment that smolders in all women, was beginning to
rival the fear and hatred that I saw in Granddaddy. At
least the anger of men counted.

Where my new friend took to the pageant life with
the same fearlessness that propelled her to jump into the
Waccamaw, I was becoming an anxious child. In addition to dresses and bows, I needed professional photographs taken for some pageants. I cried so much at the
prospect, Mom had to sneak my cat into sessions inside
her pocketbook. Midnight, I called her. A black stray
taken in after a neighbor ran over our ginger tabby and
left it in a black garbage bag with a note of minor apol-

ogy. My brothers teased she would be bad luck, or that I must be a witch to have her devotion. She followed me around and slept curled up beneath Bandit's chin under our kitchen table. My mom was brought to fits of sneezing by her presence, along with a bill from the pediatrician when my brother Jason caught cat-scratch fever from her tiny sharp claws.

On mornings before local pageants, Mom lifted me to sit on the bathroom counter and have my hair bound in thin heated rollers. The bathroom door was left open so we could hear the morning TV we usually watched in bed. In the mirror, I could see my hair in sideways loops that made even rows of steaming pink rubber, each bubble of wispy brown resembling hollow circles of the cool brass knuckles my dad kept on the dresser. The sharp stink of burning hair and a cloud of Aquanet hovered under the vanity lights. "Being beautiful is painful. It's work," Mom said. Most of what I retain about particular pageants comes from pictures of me with numbers pinned to the hem of a dress. In what would have been one of the first, my dress looks borrowed and too big. I cannot tell if I am really smiling or if the lipstick has smeared. I can feel my mom and Midnight out of the frame. What sticks out to me is the getting ready and the embarrassment of walking around afterward in all that makeup. In a dress made to draw attention when I wanted it the least. The feeling of deep shame heating my whole body, as if there were another me filled with fire standing right beside me like a red shadow. We usually went to Nana's house afterward, as we did after everything, and it was a favorite thing, even all dressed up, to walk in and find the living room full of my dad and his brothers in the mood to tell stories. These stories were recollected among the brothers over and over, as we asked them to repeat the stories of Drunken Jack, Alice Flagg, Blackbeard. And just as we asked them, they asked their mama for her stories. Nana was the ultimate keeper. Her sons were freer in their telling, but she knew everything.

I remember walking up her patio after one pageant, stepping on the fallen pink of crape myrtle petals, and hearing for the first time one particular story. The squish of the teal shag under my shoes, the smell of coffee, butter beans, Nana's perfume. My brothers playing under nobody's supervision, as Dad and Uncle Les debated something only Nana could clarify.

"Mama, I wanna know more about this trial," said Leslie, her middle son, blond and blue-eyed like her. It must have been the year the TV movie came out about it, but that would place it on the edge of too late. In 1978, Nana had been a juror on the trial for one of South Carolina's then most-famous murderers, Rudolph Tyner. A made-for-TV movie that followed the son of one of his victims, *Vengeance: The Story of Tony Cimo*, aired in 1991. She and the other jurors were sequestered at a roadside motel next to the courthouse in Conway. The day she got picked for duty, the sheriff, Junior Brown, escorted her home from the courthouse and told her to pack a suitcase under his supervision. He wouldn't let her talk to anybody.

"Les, you know I can't talk to you about it, son." Her voice stretched high when she got upset. The trial itself had been years ago, but she maintained that she could not breach confidence, though I suspect it was an excuse not to talk about it. Not to think about it even a little. She told me that the only time she feared for her life was in the room with Rudolph Tyner.

"He was a mean fella and he just stared right at you." My uncle had her going now. "He was guilty as I don't know what. I watched their son, that Tony Cimo, go at that New York boy Tyner right in the courtroom. Just jumped at him. But now once he got put on death row, you remember what happened?" she was asking her sons, but I was wide-eyed and hooked.

Tyner would be murdered on death row by the most famous serial killer the state has yet produced, a man who claimed before his execution to have raped and murdered at least a hundred women. The first woman he abducted was a hitchhiker. He left her for dead in a swamp, though she was living still and managed to crawl out, and he boasted it was the best night of his life. "Well, Pee Wee Gaskins, he was already on death row." She had her storytelling rhythm going, matching her sentences with the rocks of her chair. "He was a real famous serial killer. And this boy Tony Cimo hired him to kill Tyner before he was supposed to be executed by the state. Now, Gaskins had this radio that Tyner was

always asking to borrow. I guess he must have heard him
playing it from his cell. Well, Gaskins fixed this radio up
as a bomb, and when Tyner turned it on, it exploded and
killed him. Blew his head off, I reckon."

Nobody was listening except me, I realized. Dad and
his brothers had asked her about it, and then gone outside to check on the boys. I knew they had really gone out
for cigarettes. How different would her stories have been
if she'd had girls instead of more Jones boys? Would the
repetitions she was asked for be less violent? She must
have known that I was always listening to her even then.
"You don't want to hear me talk so much," she said on
the phone, after years of Granddaddy's abuses and her
sons' walking away. "Nana, that's why I call." Remembering is survival, and beauty the easiest faith.

I walked back to the Doll Room to change clothes.
"I started collecting because I never had any daughters,"
she told me, the longing still in her voice forty years after
she started collecting these dolls in the mid-1970s. Her
friend Tommy took her to a showroom up in Columbia,
where, surrounded by stick-straight models of costumed,
expressionless, and tiny women, something clicked for
her and she filled an empty bedroom with walls full of
them. These dolls were shells as empty as the whelks my
hermit crab outgrew, but to her each one was a life she
might have had, a crinolined cipher into which she could
imagine an escape. By the time I was born, she had hundreds of them displayed in glass cases lining the walls
of the Doll Room, a bedroom that, when her boys were

old enough and she had abandoned her dream of daughters, she carpeted in the shag of the era in pink. A deep near-purple orchid. The walls were not papered, but they might as well have been done up in yellow. The love seat was a print of butterflies and flowers, and sat under the brief window that separated the two display cases filled with the other lives she might have led. There were the president's wives. A series of fairy-tale girls, their size and form no different than the grown women like Mrs. Lincoln. Little Red Riding Hood with her tiny wicker basket, and Cinderella, who wore blue. The dolls were a small liberty for Nana, though they felt sad and caged to me. Nana sometimes bought two of the same doll, one for her and one for me. On top of the carbon-copy collection she was giving me, she reminded me consistently that I would inherit hers one day. "I don't know what you're gonna do with all these dolls," she'd say.

Did going back over this violence she was summoned to judge make her feel safer? I wonder. What she suffered was nothing compared with the bloody evidence left behind by murderers and serial killers. At least her husband was not a killer. I imagine she also liked being treated as an adult. Having a job, however gruesome, after being forced to quit hers as a bank teller decades before just because my granddaddy wouldn't have a wife of his working. Jury duty gave her a real reason to leave her house.

One raining gray day after school, Mom drove us to a seamstress's house. I looked out the window, noting that the blur of pinewoods flying past was only broken up by trailers and the strewn contents of their yards. Faded plastic wading pools filled with fallen leaves, a few painted wooden signs with PSYCHIC or PALM READING painted on, and speedboats propped upon cinder blocks in the yards. The drizzle had not let up, and a favorite thing to do when it was raining and Mom was speeding was to roll the window halfway down and stick my hand out, to feel the drops of rain as stinging needles pricking my palm. I can't deny that even then some of my hurt was self-inflicted and sought. Nana already sat at a kitchen table with a mug of black coffee in her hand, and she chatted easily with the seamstress, as she could with anyone.

"Can't we go with something a little lighter? Maybe a pink?" Nana asked, after the seamstress held a deck of reds and oranges against me. Nana had the checkbook, willingly given over by her husband for a grandkid who didn't belong to Mike. Mom and Nana went through yards of fabric. More tulle and lace. Opalescent polyester. Beading and sequins. I stood on a little box while layers of cloth were draped over each shoulder. Pins stuck into my sides, holding folds and creases together. I knew well by this fitting how to bear the discomfort of smiling politely when you'd most like to cry from fear or, more often, anger.

The morning before my last pageant, Mom and I picked up Nana from her house and we set out for Columbia. We passed the street famous in Conway for a fat

oak tree that stands in the center of the road, unaware
of its odd placement. As old as the Declaration of Independence. The city paved around its history rather than
raze it. George Washington could have stopped here to
unscroll a papyrus map and double-check his directions
on the way to King's Highway. When my dress had been
finished, Nana arranged for a professional portrait to
be made of me wearing it. A pink bodice and layer-cake
tiers of marshmallow skirt. A matching pink bow for
my hair. Lipstick and blush. Midnight the cat unseen in
the picture purring away on my lap. This pageant was
much bigger than the ones I'd been doing around town.
Several hundred little girls were entered in this one,
and there would be several phases to this competition.
A swimsuit competition was tacked on, and little girls
were expected to strut around more than half-naked for
a bunch of grown men with nowhere else to be in the
middle of the day. On the family piano, the one Nana
bought from Uncle Jack for me to have lessons, there is
a photograph of me in a white one-piece with a red rose
and some rhinestones hot-glued up the straps. I'm all
done up in paints and powders, posing with one hand on
a not-yet-there hip and fuming behind a smile.

Though I would be judged on my appearance in a
bathing suit the next day, it did not occur to me yet to
worry about the shape and size of my body. Both Mom
and Nana constantly dieted, and it became my brothers and me who reminded and sometimes begged our
mom to eat. Most of my childhood she lived off saltine

crackers with peanut butter and Coca-Cola. Even as I watched them shield themselves from the crude jibes of men and the sneering insults of other women by making themselves smaller, I couldn't help but understand that they wanted some part of themselves to disappear. Nana claimed to diet more than she seemed to lose weight. She was always eating a piece of cake or white bread with butter. "I shouldn't be eatin' this, but it's so good. It'll ruin my figure," she said but with a giggle and a wink. The joke was that she was fat already, which she wasn't. Granddaddy liked her always thinner, as if he wanted to make her so small she'd shrink herself gone one day. She liked to share with me her happy memories of their marriage, as if trying to say that it wasn't always all bad. To convince herself. Granddaddy would often promise her something new and expensive if she lost a certain amount of weight. Many of her most prized, most valuable possessions were acquired after weeks or months of fasting on grapefruit or cabbage-soup diets from women's magazines she had in a pile by her rocking chair. She interpreted her prizes as appreciation for her body, though I cannot help but see them as packaging to wrap around his perfect-looking wife when they went out to business or family events, before going home and raising a hand. No wonder she loved these accessories that were shown off at public events. He treated her halfway better out in public.

"Now, one year, I lost fifty pounds, and he bought me a fur coat. Sometimes he'd say, 'Jackie, if you lose thirty pounds by December, I'll buy you a diamond,' which he did," she said with pride I couldn't take away. "You know you're always beautiful to us, Nana," I told her. It was true. I saw in pictures how she'd aged, but they never seemed to reflect the woman I knew well. My memory replaces her white hair with flaxen blond, her hearing aid with big gold clip-on earrings.

At the pageant, I remember sitting backstage and sweating under the weight of heavy makeup. The dizzy sweet smell of hairspray so thick that the residue glued all the fallen sequins and sloughed-off powder to the floor. A scent oddly metallic that gave me a headache and brought me back to a scene from a hunting trip to Marion with Dora and her family. Miss Dorothy asked us to convey something to Dora's father out in their shed, and we skipped off in obedience. Dora seemed not to notice the sprays and streams of red across the concrete floor, but I recalled watching little red shoe prints appear where she walked over to her father, who was dressing a deer he'd shot. The buck's decapitated head hung from a hook on the ceiling. Drops of red dripped from the fur on what used to be its neck but was now only ragged, dangling skin leading up to open eyes. Blood dripped, and ended in tiny splashes on the floor that seemed as if they would be loud but were not loud at all. Is that even how you skin and dismember a deer? Dressing it by undressing it one layer at a time. The images have merged perhaps with scenes from the horror movies I watched with my brothers and cousins that I should not have been watching. In the back seat of the car on the way back to Myrtle Beach, I declared myself done for good with pageants.

Dora and other classmates still competed in those pageants, but I began telling anybody who would listen that I would go to college. It must have seemed a boast as grating as crinolines in so young a kid, but the part of me that still clung to fairy tales and ghost stories knew the power of repetition, and so I reminded myself as often as I could. For Nana especially, her education had guaranteed nothing, perhaps even was a mark against marriageability. What Southern man wanted a wife who knew more than he did and had a piece of paper to prove it? I wanted that piece of paper and the freedom it offered. I was told once by a cousin, "Your brothers can go to college." And by Granddaddy, "Your husband will go to college."

Nana had a pageant portrait made for my parents. For years, it hung over Uncle Jack's old piano, over the smaller picture of me in my competition bathing suit. A couple of feet tall, it took some strength for me, at sixteen, to remove from its place on the wall and tear the heavy portrait paper in half and then into little pieces. Sweating and sticky afterward, the rhythm of tearing and breaking so soothing. The broken glass cut my hands and that felt good, too, like when I used to stick my hand out the car window and catch spikes of rain in my palm. It felt like the only way to extricate myself from the patterns I saw around me. Stories, like anger and ghosts, come more alive with every repetition. Almost all stories, unlike memories, are told in the predictable rise and fall of tumescence. Men imagining what has fallen into their laps. Here we chuck out Aristotle in favor of the forms of women who tell stories shaped like themselves that history made a point of forgetting. The stories of women, like their bodies and lives, are fuller, rounder, softer. Prone to repetition. Like love. Like songs. Like ghosts.

Take, for instance, the ghost of a woman known as both Mary and the Lady in White. The Lady in White is said to still be seen running into the waves on nights when the moon is full. There's a boat tour out to Edingsville Beach to try to catch sight of her. She lived in a beachfront cottage on that remote end of Edisto Island, with her husband, a fisherman who spent long stretches at sea in the 1880s. As you may have seen coming, unlike poor Mary and the rest of the island, a hurricane had its eye on our lovely coast with its eyelashes of sea oats. She knew, as the wives of sailors just know, that her husband's ship had sunk, and at first light after the storm's passing, she raced to the beach and saw, however improbably, the body of her husband floating beyond the waves. She was last seen running into the surf to retrieve his body and is herself accounted thereafter drowned. Dragged under by the storm's riptide or her own grief. Without a husband, what was there to live for, I guess is the moral of the story.

6

The Ferry or the Road?

I ACCOUNT IT PAST TIME TO HIT THE ROAD AND get out of Myrtle Beach for a while. How easy to get stuck there, even on the page. We are on our way to Charlotte, the Queen City, named for a queen of Britain, where downtown is called uptown and the ghosts are friendly.

Ah, but how to leave home. It is always harder than you think. Presently, I wonder which route to show. Every going is different, though crossing the river is easier these days. When Nana was a girl, as she would say, and she and her family traveled from High Point, North Carolina, where her daddy worked for a time in the fur-

niture business, to Myrtle Beach—no. I will let her tell it.
"When I was a girl," she liked to tell, "and you wanted
to go to the beach with your family, you took an oxcart
to the flat ferry, down at Peachtree Landing, and you sig-
naled the ferryman by hitting a piece of metal that was
hanging off a tree branch against a plowshare that somebody had strung up." I heard this account from her more
than once, though the first railroad to Conway from the
other side of the river opened in 1900. River crossings
were at Socastee for the Waccamaw and Galivants Ferry
for the Pee Dee. The railroad went over Withers Swash,
where children would learn their swimming strokes
and fished for flounder. *Swash* means as a verb to move
with violence or bluster, and as a noun, it is a narrow
channel of water between sandbanks. Easy to see how
swashbuckling came to be applied to pirates. During the
height of Prohibition, a boat from Canada was trying
to sail around the Volstead Act, as so many did. The
coast was full of rum-runners for the same reasons that
it appealed to the pirates of the Golden Age. The net-
work of inlets and rivers made hiding out easy. Like the
Capitana, the *Planter*, and many more, this Canadian
ship sank in a storm between the shore and the horizon. A partial list of known shipwrecks along the Low
Country includes the *Lucy Ann*, the *Horace Greely*, the
Peace and Harmony, *Queen of the Wave*, *Gem of the
Sea*, and *Freeda A. Wyley*, whose broken limbs stick
out of the sand at Forty-third Avenue. Hidden by the
dunes, between shadows of wax myrtle and sea oats,

up to the line of dry soft sand the waves hauled from their churning depths cases and cases of wine and spirits that had belonged moments before to the cargo hold of this nameless ship. The townsfolk of Myrtle Beach spread the word among households as they might news of a hurricane, and brought lanterns and blankets to the beach for a great party the night the alcohol washed up. When it wasn't the Joneses, it was someone else supplying first one vice, then another.

It was the poorer folks like Nana's parents who took the river ferry. A Hardee by birth, she never remembered or mentioned the ferryman, so I will have to improvise after he arrives, as we stand on the riverbanks with our coins in hand, waiting. There Charon appears, guarding this swampy bank, returning those who have pulled a golden bough off a backyard branch. Very nearly the Styx itself. Water black with its own memories. Of dinosaurs. Of the Waccamaw. Of greedy, sickly conquistadors. Of privateers, hired to build settlements by the king of an island far away, who shot a bear for food and called their first outpost Bear Bluff. Of the broken bones of redcoats tricked by Francis Marion, and the ghosts of the hurricane drowned. Is there not another river, besides this most obvious one? The river of forgetting, where spirits wait to be born again in words on pages.

We will not take the ferry, I think. The route via highway is nearly parallel, so let's hit the road. Every two or three months, Mom packed the silver station wagon and piled us into the car for the four-hour drive from

Myrtle Beach to visit her family up in Charlotte. Dad rarely came on these visits, only for the annual Christmas Day drive and sometimes not even then. Dad kissed the crowns of our heads before we hopped inside Mom's car with coloring books and little plastic toys from McDonald's. He'd then walk around to the driver's side and my parents would say things too low for me to hear, though I tried hard to listen. After a kiss on her lips, he walked back into the little brown house to give either his brothers or Uncle Jack a call, and Mom backed out of the driveway with a swish of pampas grass, which is better for looking than for touching. The fronds will slit open palms and bare feet so that the sandy earth is soaked in blood before you feel the sting. Mom relaxed when we pulled away from the neighborhood, I could tell. Already I didn't need to worry about her as much. We were soon to be with Grandpa, and I would be halfway free for a few days to be a kid with my brothers.

He raised Mom and her siblings alone after his wife chose her native country and the cool, wet metropolis of London, England, over the sticky, malarial heat of the South. They met at a dance hall in London when Grandpa was stationed near Heathrow in the Air Force, where, as an aviation engineer, his mechanical engineering skills made him too valuable to ship to the fighting in Korea. He loved to dance, for which he had little rhythm or memory for steps, but he did not shy away from looking foolish if he was having fun. May, my maternal grandmother, my English grandmother, the grand-

mother I met only twice, was as good as he was bad on
the dance floor. He sold her and her friends contraband
cigarettes that he'd smuggled from the base. His first
business, really, lifting cartons of American cigarettes
and selling them to English addicts still on postwar aus-
terity. Grandpa spun her around and around that night
they met until she was dizzy enough to marry him.

May was named for the month she was born, the second in a trio of cousins named for all the spring months.
She stood five feet tall, but was no less glamorous for it.
A redhead with memories of Hitler's Blitz, of hiding out
in the Tube tunnels and sleeping in hammocks strung
over the tracks. An unexploded mortar bomb was discovered in her sister's garden in the 1960s, and all the
children, including my mom and aunts and uncle, were
evacuated. Eventually May chose queen and country and
rusted-out bombs to the active ones of her marriage. After a decade of isolation that led to shameful and hushed
breakdowns and whispers of whirlwind affairs, taking
off to take care of herself was the best she could do for
her four kids. Of her infidelity, Grandpa borrowed the
stiff upper lip of his in-laws. "She ran off with the milk-
man," he said sometimes. He always drove me to the
airport when it was time for me to return to my New
York graduate school, and on predawn drives down Billy
Graham Parkway, he'd remember taking May down the
same road to catch her final flight to London. He'd just
started a business selling gates and clocks to local businesses. Repairing the mystical hands that mark time's

passage always seemed a magical gift to me. It is not just anybody who knows how to travel through past and future, to define what is the present. He had made a deal with May. If Carolina Time, as he called his business, failed, he'd bring the kids over to England, and they'd all start over across the pond. Getting out of the car at the airport curb, instead of "Good luck with your dream" or "Thanks for watching the kids," she looked him in the eye and said, "I hope you fail." He marked that as the moment that drove him to succeed, but he was always going to succeed. I wondered at first upon hearing this story who would want to live without the loving kindness of my grandpa. That she had the freedom to leave at all, to imagine a life outside of her marriage, must have been seen as an act of generosity on his part instead of a simple choice on hers.

I knew May mostly through boxes of British chocolates and strong black tea she shipped to Mom regularly, the Union Jack on the packaging reminding me of Nana's British doll, with the tall fuzzy hat. Mom's half Englishness was masked by her Southern accent, but for the cups of PG Tips and Twinings loaded with milk and cubes of sugar that were excellent for stacking into replicas of the Tower of London and Windsor Castle. I traveled to meet May once, when I was five. Grandpa offered to pay for his daughters to visit their mother, to bring one child along, and my strongest recollection of her is of a trip to the beach at Brighton. The carnival along the wooden boardwalk reminded me of the spinning rides at the Pavilion, but the weather was cold and leaden. No humidity or peaking blue sky. May led me down to the beach, which I could hardly believe was covered in smooth flat stones. She let me fill shopping bags full of rocks to show my brothers, and they became too heavy for either of us to lift. My other memories from the trip are less trustworthy. I may have gotten lost in the hedge maze at a famous castle, and it is possible, though less so, that I ran my fingertips over giant lily pads in a room made of glass. These scenes are mixed up with the souvenir-booklet photographs that Mom and her sisters returned with, and whose pictures I pawed through near-daily for years, until they were lost when we moved from the little brown house, along with the corn snake that slipped out of Jason's aquarium a few weeks before moving day and that Mom never bothered looking for. He escaped every now and then, and I pressed towels between the carpet and door so he couldn't crawl into my room, checked under my pillow and blankets before sleep, and took flashlight rays to the darkness of my book bag until he was recovered. I have wondered since if the future residents discovered him coiled in a shoe or in a drawer. Last time I drove by the house, I should have knocked on the door to ask. Wherever we lived, on mornings when I had a test at school, Mom made me a strong cup of Assam tea, and I built castle turrets out of sugar cubes and plopped into my cup in milky splashes the bricks of battlements.

Back in the station wagon leaving Conway for Charlotte, we all sang to the radio, my little brothers and me, with our hands and sometimes our heads out the windows, leaving town on the two-lane highway that winds past the Witch Links golf course, which the Joneses did not own. The sign at the front entrance was carved out of a half-moon of wood. A long-haired crone, cloaked and draped doubly in Spanish moss, a long, needling finger pointing from her whittled and painted hand. Mom would be singing, too, by then. Usually too reserved to do it in front of Dad, the real singer. Singing was life, and we brought him with us when we lamented in lyrics problems we were too young to understand. Our long weekends away, Dad recorded demos in the garage on cassette tapes, before going out to Drunken Jack's or getting roped into one of Uncle Jack's trips.

It was as if we had permission to be ourselves in the car. Or was it only after the river crossing, over the newer concrete bridge? We passed the sign for the ferry landing at Galivants Ferry, but I wouldn't go looking for the plowshare for just about anything down by that water. On through Marion, where my school friend Dora and her family had their hunting cabin. Marion, that village an hour inland from Conway, farther than Cool Spring, and all cotton farms and crumbling old sharecroppers' shacks. It is a location that will come to play a larger part in my family's story, so we'll take the liberty of pretending that on at least one drive to see Grandpa, I had the prescience to take notice of a wide empty field on the northbound side of Highway 501 where lay the future fortunes of the Joneses. Marion the town and the county were named after Francis Marion, the local war hero. In school we had learned that Marion, the "Swamp Fox" as he was commonly known, led a guerrilla war against the British during the American Revolution. George Washington himself was supposedly a big fan, and Marion was rumored to have been quite popular with the colonial ladies, who could not resist the man who strategically led British soldiers to death by snakebite, alligator bite, or mosquito bite in the malarial swamps. Marion was descended from French Huguenots who fled Europe after Louis XIV, the Sun King, declared Calvinism off-limits. Some of these French Calvinists voyaged abroad to South Carolina. Horry County was named after the Huguenot Peter Horry, another pal of Washington's.

As long as we are on the road, why not take a small detour so readers can see another tourist attraction. "The Holy Ghost is the only ghost welcome here," reads the old-timey white scrawl on a wooden sign in front of All Saints Church off King's River Road in Murrells Inlet. While I hate to call anyone a liar, much less on church property, that is just not the truth. The Gray Man is seen not too far from the old Wachesaw plantation that's now a golf course and gated housing development where Uncle Leslie lives with his family. In the South, manners are wielded like crucifixes at an exorcism. As if it weren't clear who is welcome where in South Carolina. I suppose politeness works some magic on small demons.

This is a land where the languid Spanish moss sways on the strong arms of Southern live oaks that waltz in the kaleidoscopic heat haze, and the air is so thick, it holds up the whispers that would elsewhere collapse. The conditions are right. Continuity and silence, according to Wharton, and we've got plenty of both. *Wachesaw*, in the language of the Waccamaw tribe, means "place of great weeping." Every place sees its share of tears. Then again, there are those places where the guilt is not glued down by the tree sap. In school each spring, my class took a field trip to Brookgreen Gardens, which lies to the south of Wachesaw in Murrells Inlet. It is advertised as a great sculpture garden. A Grand Strand attraction with a petting zoo for the kids and annual light festivals. I, too, am guilty of taking out-of-towners to spot alligators from pontoon boats and to walk between the electrified wings of oak-size butterflies. The grounds are an impressionist blur of moss green on gray and brown tree bark, azalea bushes in magentas and bubble-gum pinks, white marble and oxidized copper that ooze together atop the blue. Images and feelings evoked clearer than history. Naked Dianas hunting. A wood nymph here and there. Dionysus with some wine. Two stallions fighting in a fountain, for some reason. After one field trip, in the eighth grade, my history teacher divided the classroom into small groups, and after distributing buckets and sticks, we were instructed to imagine we were enslaved Africans pummeling the hull off rice, and yet I do not recall learning the legacy of the grounds. Not one, but four rice plantations owned by Joshua Ward, who is accounted the largest slaveholder in American history. On an 1860 ledger, among his estate's holdings are listed 1,130 people in his possession. It is difficult to look at the marsh water, too dark for divining, and not feel the heaviness of tears, bodies, curses cast into its mud, even now which folks ignore between exhibits about the sculptures and wildlife.

We find ourselves next cruising through the flatlands of tobacco and cotton fields, with the swamps and their ghosts in the rearview mirror. Cue the Judds and Dwight Yoakam, Reba and Willie, Loretta and Conway. We all sang happily in and out of sync, never on or even near any key, until we passed the Columns, the white plantation outside Florence surrounded by trailers and locals sitting in beach chairs on their lawns with shotguns in their laps and Confederate flags disfiguring further such scenes. This was where the drippy moss disappeared from the tree limbs, and the air began to feel less fraught. The branches robed in webworms groped at the edges of the car here. One time Mom and I were driving at this point in the road under a sky that shone blue and rays of sun over one lane and poured rain across the other. "The devil must be beating his wife," she said. Making it through this stretch, we came to the NASCAR racetrack in Darlington and could keep on with the deep and palliative croons of whoever was on the radio forever and ever amen until we pulled into Grandpa's driveway in Charlotte. Before Mom could pull the key from the ignition, the boys and I bounded barefoot down the hill of rough, sun-hot driveway and into his arms. Who could pause to tie shoes with excited, clumsy fingers when he was waiting for us? Here I am feeling greedy for the next memory that I retrieve, rewind, and replay by choice for a change. One wherein I am enfolded in blissful safety and lifted spinning from the burning summer pavement as kid laugher floats over a chorus of cicadas and ice cubes clink the edges of a glass of bourbon. I was always the first to be picked up and held aloft. He smelled of the bourbon he drank out of a wax Dixie cup, vetiver-laced cologne, shoe leather, and oak trees, which were taller and whose limbs seemed to climb upward instead of in the crooked sprawl of home. Lightning bugs danced between dusky peach rays of twilight, and I kissed his cheek. I could taste the salt of sweat and feel his calm, openhearted authority.

Atop the red-brick patio, Grandpa stood in sagging khakis and canvas boat shoes and nothing else but his glasses. He clapped his hands together while we double-hopped the steps to reach him. "Hey, kiddos!" He pulled the phrase out as long as his arms, which were deeply tanned and damp with sweat. On these weekends, he never wore a shirt, and his stomach ballooned over the waistband of his pants. Again we pause on the vanity of men, which grows in step with success.

His one-story brick house was an odd arrangement of hallways and living rooms that led to bedrooms and centered around a kitchen. Despite its unusual shape, it was always lively on these visits. It was also a bona fide bachelor pad, complete with a wet bar, pool table, and hot tub. He was the only adult who regarded our input as valuable as a grown-up's, while still indulging us in childhood. On summer mornings, he invited me to pick scuppernongs with him from the mass of grapevines that enshrouded a corner of his back porch. "What's your favorite subject, kid?" His question was followed by a scuppernong seed that he spit into the yard. "English," I said always, and my own scuppernong seed would fall just past my feet. He'd laugh and brush it off the side of the porch without a word. And as everybody else in the house slept in, we asked each other questions—Where did I want to go to college? What was his favorite country he'd ever been to?—and eat the vine clean.

These weekends were carefree ones of games of pool and darts in Grandpa's living room. We pretended to pour scotch on the rocks into wax-paper Dixie cups. Enjoying pretend games of doing what men did. We slept in Mom's old bedroom, starting out on floor pallets, and in a rush of fear in the presence of invisible forces, hair on limbs stood up as our dog's would in a thunderstorm. You see, we woke every night to footsteps pacing back and forth in the attic above the bedroom and the hallway. Mom heard them, too, and just how active the ghost was on nights was the usual breakfast conversation. Here, ghosts were not stories or threats, but were heard, felt, acknowledged by the adults as real.

There was no doubt that the sounds that woke us

were footsteps, the heel-toe thud-tap of a man's heavy shoes laid down to a remembered heartbeat rhythm. Some nights they would start in the attic and then sound suddenly in the brick hallway just outside our door. Grandpa bragged that he had the ability to communicate with spirits, as Dad had with dogs, and named his house ghost Harvey, like the invisible rabbit from the Jimmy Stewart movie. Though he loved to tease us as grandfathers do, and was as rational-minded as any engineer on most counts, he claimed to share his home with Harvey, having first surmised the presence of something supernatural in the house after he and his four children, then teenagers, had barely moved in. He had woken one night to his bed shaking violently and the indentation of a figure lying next to him in the sheets. He said that he was never so scared as that initial encounter, not even when piloting planes in the Air Force. He jumped out of bed and flew through the front door and drove to his office to wait for sunrise, still wearing only underwear. At three a.m., he left his four sleeping children alone to deal with whatever it was, until he came home and had a long talk with the ghost. It was his house first, after all, and Grandpa's prevailing instinct was always to befriend. If ever we were left alone, he always said, "Don't be scared. Harvey will look after you."

An aunt told stories of Harvey's most disruptive years of haunting, when he unlocked and swung open the bathroom door when she was showering or other-

wise naked. "Don't worry about Harvey," she said to
me, in a line of half tease, half comfort. "He's not mean.
He's just a pervert." Even in death, this man could not
keep his eyes and hands to himself, and I was advised
to put up with his harassment because it was felt to be
good-natured. Boys will be boys, even in the afterlife.
Were his groping ministrations on this side of the grave,
I had a feeling my aunt's advice would be about the
same, which bothered me more than the peeping habits
of some lecherous old ghost. The air in the house did
seem peculiar. Thinner. As if I could fall right through it
and straight into another dimension.

Grandpa talked aloud to Harvey when they were
alone, but I listened from behind corner walls, usually
when he rolled biscuit dough or mixed pancake batter
at the kitchen counter in the mornings. He most often
spoke to Harvey after his kids returned to their homes,
to fill the silence of an empty house. He believed Harvey
saved his life one night, making amends for the night
he scared him out of bed. The oven was turned on by
his teenage son, who then fell asleep. As Grandpa told
it, Harvey woke him with a clattering of pots and pans
and cabinet doors until he got out of bed and discovered
half the kitchen in licking, hungry flames. One evening,
after watching young people sing and cry standing over
a crumbling wall, Grandpa showed me the cities and
countries from the news on the globe that stood by his
bookcase. It must have been early winter 1989. Running
my fingers over the raised bumps of mountain chains

and the plastic line of the equator, the world seemed available to me for the first time.

If a hurricane can pick up a house and put it down whole in the next county, their swirling winds can take us back two months with ease. Their winds blow counterclockwise, after all, practically made for time travel. A different ghost has warned of disaster, and we must return to Myrtle Beach. In September 1989, the Gray Man had been spotted in Pawley's Island by more than one witness. South Carolina was preparing for the biggest hurricane since Hazel. Looking at my Rand McNally map, I could see where Hugo had blown off the violet coast of Africa and was swirling like a carnival carriage across the Atlantic, and the Gray Man had a better track record than the weatherman. Forgive my manners, but I will only tease a cordial introduction until the appointed hour of our own sighting within these pages. His true identity is unknown, anyway. Who was he before he was a solemn apparition that walks the beaches of Pawley's Island as a warning to residents to flee, to go, to live? There are several different stories, and when the time is right, you may choose whichever suits.

Everybody knows that things are about to get serious when the Gray Man shows up, and folks who wouldn't dream of evacuating their beachfront property when the State Guard knocks on their door, as they did before Hugo, saying essentially, "If you're gonna ride it out, you've gotta sign away government blame if either home or life is lost," will pack a bag and follow the blue-spiral evacuation-route signs all the way to Appalachia. They'll do that if word gets out that he's been walking the shore. Though, they say if you see him, your house will be spared, and you have only to see a strip of shore the day after a storm to know the truth. There are always a handful of beachfront homes perfectly and sporadically preserved, while the neighboring houses, as solidly built and all up on stilts, as is the law, are soaking, salty debris piles. Some houses even crack ragged and straight down the middle like a cartoon egg. Tape up the windows, bring in the bicycles and toys from the yard. Wait in line at the Scotchman to fill up the car and get a few extra gallons of gas. Are there batteries in the kitchen drawer? And where the devil are the flashlights? Fill up the bathtubs and extra buckets with tap water while it's good and running, so you can brush your teeth and flush the toilets, though I don't know that the tap water in Horry County has ever been that good. It turned all our teeth yellow.

Hugo hit as the sun went down on a muggy late-September school day in 1989. A car in a hurry to get out of town had hit a power line and knocked out our electricity early that morning. The county didn't bother to fix it. In a few hours, everybody'd be without power anyway. Our little brown house on the edge of Conway was a few miles inland of the Intracoastal Waterway, where the turn-bridge has since been replaced by a tall concrete one that looks down on it. The Waterway is still the line of demarcation separating must-evacuate from probably oughtta. Nana and Granddaddy, who could see the ocean a half mile from their house on Calhoun and King's Highway, packed a few bags of jewelry and family photos and came to ride out the storm with us. If Hugo had not been expected to come ashore as the strongest hurricane ever to hit our coast, a hurricane party would have been in order somewhere. If you're not a Baptist on a Sunday, there's not a lot that will inspire sobriety on a weekday in the Low Country, but a category-five hurricane might be one of them.

Once the power went out at our house, we got our flashlights and radios out. I remember being a little bit bored, anticipating the awe of great forces I was too young to grasp, but interpreted as fun. Like the ups and downs of the roller coasters at the Pavilion, or the thrills of ghost stories by candlelight. It was too dark to see what made all the noise outside, and there was a lot of noise outside. The adults were worried about it. Nana and Granddaddy sat on the brick hearth of our little fireplace in silence. Nana stroked her toy poodle, Tiffany, and recalled talk of finding snakes blown up into tree limbs after Hazel. Dad had gotten the poodle, to ease Nana's loneliness, from the captain of a boat called *Mistress Tiffany*, who had a pet monkey and with whom he gave moonlight tours of the inlets and marshes. They left from Drunken Jack's after the bar closed, and the monkey went around the boat collecting tips in a captain's hat.

Dad paced around the living room with a radio in

hand, and Mom kept watch over the candles. Justin, Jason, and I made a game of seeing who could hold their palm over the dreamy, dancing flame for the longest, and I won, of course. If I had been able to endure parading on stage in sequins and bathing suit, I could endure the pain of fire. Hugo came ashore a category four, the eye making landfall just above Charleston, and spawning in Conway half a dozen tornados at that darkest time right before dawn that ripped up the live oaks at Witch Links golf course a few miles down the road. We learned later that that was the freight-train sound we heard in the dark. Maybe the adults knew all along the sound of tornado winds and spared me the knowledge. My brothers slept the whole night through, as I listened to both Mom's worry and the winds.

Uncle Mike thought he would outsmart the storm and shelter to the south. He took Chris and Brian to the safety of a high-rise hotel by Charleston's harbor. Hugo's eye was projected to come ashore at Myrtle Beach, you see, and while it is usually true that most storms crook northward at the last minute for more civilized ground in North Carolina, Hugo bent south, so that Mike's instinct had taken his family right into the eye of the storm. They were okay and only got stuck in the hotel for a few days without power. Don't be fooled by the relief of an open eye above. The back end of a hurricane is the most dangerous.

Early the next morning, I crawled out of Mom's bed, leaving her and the boys asleep. Nana and Granddaddy had taken my room and were not out yet either. Dad had cranked his pickup truck and was listening to the news on the car radio with the driver's door open. I sat on his lap looking at the tender pink blisters I had earned holding my hand over the candle, as we listened to the weather forecast. It was a cool and sunny fall day. The pine forest around the perimeter of our house was still there, but every single tree was bowed down at the waist as if in supplication to the clear blue sky. "After Hugo, none of our maps worked anymore," Dad recalls.

Nearly fifty people died in South Carolina, mostly from drowning and electrocution, and for a while it was the most damaging storm ever recorded. Dad was especially hard in reminding us not to play in even the smallest puddle until about Christmas that year, much less jump in any creek or ditch water. "If the alligators or snakes don't get you, you're liable to get electrocuted." With all the flooding, the wildlife was as displaced as the humans. When we returned to school, we heard stories of gators moving into backyard swimming pools. The Swamp Fox roller coaster down in Garden City had blown away. The worst story I'd heard came from Mc-Clellanville, just outside Charleston, where the eye made landfall. I know now that the story as it was told and retold did not happen that way. That human nature is attracted to the tallest of tales, and the need to share what we have witnessed spirals into gossip of the most inconsiderate kind. And while it's true that nearly the whole town sheltered in the local high school's gym, which really did flood up to the ceiling in the middle of the night, the rumor passing among my classmates that everyone had drowned is not. I know now that nobody died in the gym that night but still on occasion hear the story passed around as if the rumor, by now the beginning of a legend, were stronger somehow than the truth. Everybody survived drowning by climbing onto the rafters, a story scary enough to need no embellishment to me, but then I am no longer a resident of the Low Country and don't reckon to be again in this life. That such tragedy might have happened was not at all that hard to believe, especially to a child's imagination. At Dora's house, weeks after the storm, we watched from her porch as a whole house floated down the Waccamaw River.

When the National Guard allowed us to cross the swing bridge, Grandpa had us go see if his beach house in Cherry Grove still stood. He'd been so fond of his own beach memories that he'd bought a duplex on stilts and rented it out part of the year. We drove past turquoise and pink beach awnings that had been shredded by the wind, the shattered signs of the popular beachwear stores that used to say EAGLES or WINGS where we bought our dollar-apiece hermit crabs, and boarded-up windows with their messages spray-painted to the storm. HUGO GO HOME was scratched on the plywood. When we got to Cherry Grove, we had to leave the silver station wagon at the end of the block and walk around puddles and piles of debris. The beach house was still standing, but under the carport was a pile of sand nearly all the way up to the ceiling. The carpet inside the house, one story off the ground, had been soaked through from storm surge lapping underneath. Where I stood had been ocean water well over my head, and as Mom did a lap around the house to assess the damage, I noticed the water line on the stilts and stairs that led up to the front door. The ocean had stretched a full block inland and had somehow returned to where it had always been, looking pleased and contented for the exercise.

Children recognize in something only their own relationship to it, and I had thought of the ocean as a friend that welcomed me into its warmth and seemed sad to see me return to land. That it was indifferent not just to my presence, but to that of whole towns and families, was a new consideration. It swallowed whole the pier I fished from and tore in half the walls of hotels whose pools I snuck into, and it was not bothered a bit. This was an initiation into the logic of coastal life, an acceptance that danger was inevitable. Just as it is impossible to predict where the eye will make landfall, none of my family would have guessed that for the next hurricane that graces these pages, we'd be living on the north end of the Low Country.

7

_____

Aces over Eights

THE SUMMER AFTER HUGO, THE SUMMER OF 1990, my parents decided to make the move to Tennessee so Dad could sing country music on the radio. The Pancake House could do without Dad, and Waccamaw Academy would be shutting down at the end of the next school year. The inland tourists, the rubberneckers, the college kids, the Canadians, they were good for nothing but traffic and trouble. Among the locals, those who were taking their forever spots on the rebuilt pier with the other old men who fished every morning at dawn, who had played baseball for the Myrtle Beach High School Seahawks with my dad, who had lost something important to the ocean's surf and surge as we all had, swirled a mix of disdain and deference to those out-of-towners.

My parents did not want to end up like them. They had their own dreams to go after instead of giving up their time to the fantasies of these outsiders. Don't you always end up hating most those you need to stay afloat? The tourist tips added up to not much. Glued to the tabletops with globs of Country Crock and spilled maple syrup, besides. These folks didn't need my dad to scramble their eggs and deliver their hangover waffles. In Mom's ruffled peach apron and his favorite baseball cap, he did that for us on his days off, with a perfected flair I mistook for magic instead of routine. Hope infects the smallest first. My little brothers and I divined the big time in the crystal balls of our parents' eyes.

When he was at work in the mornings, I liked to hide in his guitar case. He kept the guitar propped up on a metal stand if he wasn't going out with it. When he got up from the couch, he held the fragile neck of it down at his side, like he was holding the hand of a sleeping child. The instrument seemed to follow him around more faithfully than the dog. Laid flat and left open on the carpet, I was more fascinated by the case, and when I could get away with it, would tiptoe into its empty body. The lining, a soft gray fuzz, welcomed me inside. I slunk down until my form had curled and contorted just right. The shape of that guitar case was made for the curve of my back. Smells of Camels, leather, and wood polish stayed on the fabric, softer and denser than Nana's shag carpet. The metallic whiff left by the capo and the cash he kept rubber-banded in rolls behind a trap door in the neck of the case. While we were gone, he'd take out his earnings and rustle through the leafy bills, mostly ones, and spend it on whiskey and those copper energy bracelets that regulate the ions in your immune system and keep your aura fresh or some such. Around this time, he was working on a love song called "Sam Loves Sally," a simple story about two teenagers falling in love. It never sold. The hard knocks that would give him his best material for the outlaw-country songs that did sell were still a few years away.

For my parents, still young and beautiful, three kids and a mortgage before thirty must have started to weigh. The novelty that buoys love had become worn. A life that belonged to their parents. Their friends in Nashville were childless couples whose nights were filled with jam sessions, juke joints, and cheap drugs laced with baking soda. The anticipation of the move united them in new possibility. Real estate is a known salve for marital staleness. They had never even been on a honeymoon, pregnant with me as they were. They'd eloped one weekend to the Great Smoky Mountains, and their witnesses were my uncle Leslie and his then-wife Linda. When they drove away in Dad's white Mazda pickup truck, the newlyweds found the winding roads of October Appalachia flooded with a thick, impenetrable fog. They couldn't see what was ahead, and so they stopped the car and waited. Dad, I'm sure, felt protective of his brandnew wife and his coming baby, with the imperative only a twenty-four-year-old man can feel, an emotion I have seen fire up and then pass in my brothers as they've hit twenty-five. Still I can't help but see something in this approach to the unknown: their first journey as a family bound together by God and the law was too hesitant, too tentative to charge ahead. Their instinct was to idle and wait for a clear path, and they were young enough to expect the appearance of one. How do I know all this? From Nana, of course. She collected the love stories of everyone she knew like she did her romance novels.

On their house-hunting trips, heading up to Tennessee, they usually set off in the late afternoon, preferring always to drive at night. Even now, I attribute a preference for dawn departures to the childhood fear of pitch-dark drives through back-country roads. Looking out a window into shadows and tendrils of Spanish moss, which were comforting to me in the daylight, but too like the uneven, hanging robes of ghosts at night. Webworm tents transformed into groping hands after dark, and leaves caught midfall in the sticky gossamer could sometimes become the face of an evil plat-eye, the swamp ghost stolen and used carelessly by schoolchildren to scare. That last time they went to Nashville that spring of 1990, they'd already looked at a house they wanted to put an offer on. Things were being finalized. My parents plowed into this new decade, the one that felt like it was heading toward their true destiny, with all the determination they should have used to part that fog on the Blue Ridge Parkway back in 1982. Dad had lit out of our driveway with the unshakable confidence of a man who knows that fate's got his back and his mom's got the kids.

I remember being bored with the goodbyes. Mom's blood-red canna flowers stretching toward the sun. Many years later, walking down a street in India, I caught sight of the exact shade of these canna flowers in the vermilion powder parting a married woman's hair. Memory plays tricks like that. When you're as far away from your past as you can possibly put yourself, that's when some sound or smell taps into the senses and unexpectedly knocks you back to where you came from. But I remember also begging to go with them, Mom tucking me in one of the twin beds in the Boys' Bedroom, the bed on the left where my great-grandmother May Ella died in her sleep when I was four. My only real memory of her is being held on the couch, thinking she looked like the oldest person on earth, and running away from her to hide behind the curtains. I can say I remember being held in the arms of a grandmother who was not counted a person enough to vote for the first third of her life. Dad had gone to get her for coffee, walking the length of Nana's hallway, the one still lined with repaired wedding portraits, baby pictures, and half a dozen cross-stitchings of the "Serenity Prayer" surrounded by slightly too square Easter lilies. She'd gone to God sometime in the night. Unlike Grandpa, Granddaddy would have nothing so imaginative or uncontrollable as a ghost in his house, and May Ella has remained at rest, it seems, no doubt happy to be gone. She hated my Granddaddy, even after she moved in with them. She dipped snuff her whole life, and at the supper table, Granddaddy said as he watched her place tobacco behind her lip, "May Ella, none of the women in my family dip snuff."

"Ralph, none of the men in my family are horse thieves," she replied, the only one in the house who dared talk back. My dad and his brothers stared till food fell from their open mouths, and Granddaddy got up to leave the table.

Again, I'm convinced my memory has it wrong about the night my parents left. Why wasn't I in the Doll Room? The night Mom kissed my forehead. "I want to go," I hear myself. Never before did I care to go on one of their scouting missions, but my presence seemed urgent, our separation not an option. And the anxiety must have been brewing for a while, or else Mom was feeling alarmingly sentimental, because she had a parting gift at the ready. A bunny with a purple ribbon tied around her neck. I kept that rabbit for so many years, the plastic heart glued to its fur eventually fell off. That lavender ribbon is still probably between Nana's couch cushions. Maybe in her drawer of hair clips, with the real tortoise-shell combs. Violet was a shade she complained of never being able to wear. She didn't think it necessary to tell us exactly what had happened to our parents when they failed to return on time.

Mom was in the passenger seat on the way back from Nashville to Myrtle Beach, with a pillow over her knees. Dad in his Drunken Jack's baseball cap and aviators. A

Camel cigarette unspooling between the fingers of his left hand, the side where he keeps the nails clipped for fretting. He prefers to grow his fingernails as guitar picks on the other hand, though I'm sure the floorboards of the car were speckled with his plastic picks. Tuned into that lull that descends on the return leg of all road trips. That truck had done the drive so many times, it could practically steer itself. The junctions of I-40 around Knoxville remain jumbled. Too many lanes, too much concrete all at a crook in winding roads. Knoxville is a trucking hub where tractor-trailers enter the highway in a steady flow of commerce. For years, I assumed the driver must have been drunk, the wreck the deadly consequence of carelessness or the karma of alcohol. And he was. Drunk enough to fall asleep at the wheel. Mom noticed the guy first. An eighteen-wheeler flying between lanes and cars like a pinball. "We were coming down a hill, and he was swerving all over the place. I remember saying, 'He's liable to hit somebody,' and then he hit everybody."

As my parents descended in their eastbound lane, the eighteen-wheeler zigzagged through the westbound lane of traffic, heading straight for the station wagon that I knew from dance recitals, trips to Grandpa's house, and backseat sing-alongs. Straight for my parents. He hit car after car, killing somebody on his side of the divide before busting through the concrete barrier. Between my parents and this behemoth was a teal Chevy Monte Carlo. My mother watched this car get sucked underneath the body of the truck, between the front and back wheels. She says, and I will never forget, she saw the couple duck just before the roof of the car was sheared straight off.

And that's when the engine of the truck, that terrifying face you always see riding your tail in the rearview mirror, hit my parents. It plowed into the driver's side, right into my dad, and pushed that station wagon, a Subaru that Mom credits with saving their lives, off the side of the road before coming to a halt. Again, my memory swerves sharply from reality, and I am in the back seat of the car with them just before the crash, where I almost remember begging to be, and then I am suddenly skipping into the future. I've cartwheeled across our timeline as if it weren't anything at all to time-travel— and when you're seven, I guess it's not. What I still don't know could fill the roads between South Carolina and Tennessee.

Back at the scene: cicadas clanging like church bells, ringing in the heat, and the ambulance sirens are heralding the end of Dad's ambitions, which never had the chance to really get going at all. Looking back, this was the dividing point, the separation between hope and resignation for all of us. No, maybe not resignation. That sounds too quiet to my ears, and what followed was not quiet. Anything but. The wreck, as it came to be known, lit the fuse on a spectacular detonation of giving up in both my parents. This was the showstopper, literally, or for a good long while, though life gave them a couple of disastrous encores. Cut to movie montage. Reels of

flashing lights and broken glass. Hospital gowns. Beeping heart monitors. Who knew we'd end up hearing
more than our share of heart-monitor dings in the coming years.

Nana did not tell us about the accident, but I remember the whispering. While doing headstands against the
wall, reading from her book of ghost stories, playing
with my brothers, all as she and her sister whispered,
worried, and picked up the phone. Whispers, worry,
phone. The clang of phone receiver finding its place atop
the beige rotary. A kid can sense secrecy, even if she can't
tell what's important. Jason claims that Uncle Leslie sat
us down and said there had been an accident.

I have this early memory of frying chicken with Mom,
and it starts with the sounds. Sizzles and pops. There's
the smell of flour and grease, and I am hungry. I can feel
the wall of heat from the stove. I see my legs, next to my
brother Justin's, dangle off the kitchen counter, thin and
white, wiggling like fishing bait. The edge of the counter
cuts into the back of my thighs. It must be summer, always summer, because we are both in our underwear
and nothing else, and the chemical scent of chlorine lin-
gers in my damp hair, which has turned green the few
strands of almost-blond. Always summer.

It is my turn. It is exciting. I can't see her, but I know
Mom is in the background. I pick up a raw chicken leg,
almost the color of my legs, except for patches of pink
and purple. But there are pricks in the wet, cold skin,
and the flesh does not yield quite as easily to pokes. I do

not recognize these dots as plucked feathers, but I feel them beneath my fingers, tiny and raised. I pick it up by the small end. The closer I look, the more I can see yellow underneath all the other colors. There are two grayish knots sticking out and into the pads of my fingers. I do not understand them as bone, like mine.

There is a correct order to what I'm about to do. I look to Mom. She is young and beautiful and still happy. She points at the bowl of orange, eggy swirls. I dip the chicken in. It is colder than I expect, and the egg drips in strangely strong tendrils. Next is the bowl of flour, speckled with reds and blacks of spice. I drop the chicken leg into the white powder. It makes a muted thud, and flour jumps from the bowl onto the counter. I roll the leg around, feeling the slipping drippy egg catch the soft flour. It makes a sticky sludge that coats my fingers as well as the chicken leg. And I rub my fingertips back and forth, delighting in the slick globs. What is more satisfying than a good mess? The next step is to place it on a plate, full of pieces of already flour-muddied chicken, but I see the big black cast-iron pan. It is deep with bubbling grease that looks awfully busy reaching into the air. I want to do the next part too, and badly. I wait until Mom isn't looking. My hand hovers over the pan. The gurgle of grease is hypnotic. I drop my creation into the liquid, and then I scream. Before I even recognize the pain, I hear my voice. Spots of purple-red on sickly yellow are appearing on my leg and arm, like the welts left on the raw chicken's flesh.

This image, these colors, were brought back to me when I saw Dad's leg for the first time, a couple of weeks after the accident. The scar, still inflamed, ran in a thick, jagged line up his calf and shone violet mixed with the sickly yellow of a bad storm sky. The same primordial aura as the bloody fluid on the foam tray of a pack of Tyson chicken legs or the blood that puddled in muddy pools from the deer that Dora's dad skinned. I've framed the wreck as a disaster, but they were lucky. Thank God they weren't in Dad's pickup truck, which had about the same minimal heft of our rusted swing set in the backyard. Dad spent eight days in the hospital in Tennessee. His leg was broken in seven places, the shin and ankle nearly crushed. There was talk of amputation, but in the end he had a metal plate put in his leg, to support the remaining bone, held into place by two dozen screws. The station wagon was totaled. In one of our many moves when I was in high school, I came across a Polaroid of it in the junkyard, an insurance snap maybe used in the court case against the truck driver. He'd been driving for days without a rest, popping pills to meet schedules. When his rig came to a stop, one dead and an interstate shut down completely, he hopped out of the cab and fled the scene on foot, leaving his son, who was about my age, alone in the passenger's seat.

Mom flew home a few days after the wreck. She limped out of baggage claim with crutches and a leg brace that extended from shin to thigh, with a little circle cut out over her kneecap. By some miracle, she'd only managed to tear some cartilage in her knee. Dad was driven home by a cousin. What followed was a period I hold as one of particular closeness to Dad, though the wreck must have been one of the worst things of his life. He was essentially bedridden, until he could walk with a cane. After the cast came off, he had a gel-filled boot he kept on his leg, the left one. He just wouldn't get out of bed. So we played cards. Not the poker he'd taught all of us in late-night sessions around the miniature blue Playskool table. Texas Hold'em, five-card stud. We counted our ante in Cheerios and Froot Loops. I spent hours practicing waterfall shuffles with decks as big as my hands. "Deal to the left," Dad instructed, wearing the white-banded visor whose clear green bill had a milky white scar where the plastic had been folded. I counted in clumsy swipes till we all had a hand. "Now, ante up," he'd say, as excited to win a pot of breakfast cereal as the clinking color chips we were taught to play with later.

"Mark, I wish you wouldn't smoke in here," Mom said from the couch or the kitchen at some point, to which Dad would apologize in good humor, "I'm sorry, honey," if he was winning or give an aggravated wave if he was not, in neither case putting his cigarette out.

"Too rich for my blood." I'd throw down the lingo as casually as I would fistfuls of Cheerios, just as he did, folding when I couldn't make a decent hand.

"One-eyed jacks are wild," I called if I was dealing, "and aces are low." The only hand you didn't want was aces over eights. Bad luck. Nothing so serious or important as luck to gamblers.

"It's the dead man's hand, kids," Dad said. "The hand that old Wild Bill Hickok played when somebody shot him in the back of the head."

Once the father of a neighborhood boy came to our door and demanded to speak to Dad. "You been teachin' my boy to gamble?" the prudish redneck grumbled. And my dad answered, "So what? He ain't any good at it, anyway." In some retellings of this incident, punches are thrown in the doorway, but in most, only the words are felt worth remembering. It was Nana's side of the family who dealt stories, that Dad claimed more affinity for, but gambling was in the blood of the Joneses. Granddaddy and his brothers kept a gambling house on Chester Street and had poker games in backrooms all over town. Adjoining an office, they ran a burlesque club called the Gaiety Lounge.

After the wreck, I think that Dad felt, at not yet thirty, that he'd gambled enough for his lifetime. He'd anted up big time and nearly lost the whole pot, tip and gig money, life and limb. Lying propped up on the bed, on frilly sheets of peach and blue, he taught me to play gin instead, and we played and played. "It's the same rules as poker hands but with ten cards each, and you go back and forth pulling from the deck and discarding till you get all your cards in hands of three or more."

The bluffing was better, more suited to fits of giggles. I'd pretend to be laying a card on the discard pile and at the last minute flip it over and declare, "Gin!" Little kids love nothing so much as a successful trick.

My brothers were considered too wild, too prone to the manners that went unchecked in them to be trusted so close to Dad's leg, and it was just me and Dad telling stories, playing gin. No bets, though sometimes we tallied up cards unused in losing hands to keep score.

"What do you think of your old one-legged daddy?" he asked with teasing exaggeration, but there was missing the daringness that had led him to talk back to the neighbor.

"You look like a pirate," I said, which made him laugh. The laughs you get as a child hold strong as other memories morph or recede, as stories must change to survive. It was my turn to retell to Dad the stories of my favorite pirates for him.

Gather 'round, and I will tell some more tales of the Golden Age of Pirates. We have met already the most fearsome, Blackbeard, who, before storming ships for bounty and entering battles for blood, twisted gunpowder into the ends of his beard and hair and lit the strands to look like the devil come straight from hell. Who hung no Jolly Roger from his galleon mast, but strapped for all to see a human skeleton holding an hourglass. Who blockaded Charleston Harbor for the summer of 1718 and held captive prominent Charlestonians. Stede Bonnet we know already, Blackbeard's less-competent friend and onetime partner, more of a professional acquaintance, it must be said, their workplace the high seas! I earlier left hanging the question of the Gentleman Pirate, but he was captured in a rowboat, kept in the dungeon of Charleston's Old Exchange, and hanged alongside fifty less-colorful pirates in the purges that began in 1718. Speaking of colorful, there is Calico Jack, the pirate famed for the bright and flowery prints he liked to wear, "flowerdy," Nana would say, for flying first the aforementioned flag with the skull and crossbones, for keeping not one but two lady pirates among his crew, and if they brought with them bad luck, then it was Jack who suffered it, and not the ladies.

Mary Read and Anne Bonney were the women he allowed on his sloop, the *Ranger*. They bound their breasts, dressed as men, and enlisted as privateers, before realizing they could do better and becoming pirates. When Anne's lover Captain Calico Jack was captured in Jamaica, she got a last visit with him before the execution, and instead of the comforting words of a mourning wife, she flat-out said, "Jack, if you'd fought like man, you wouldn't be getting hanged like a dog." Both women were caught, and upon sentence of death revealed that they were pregnant. Read died from childbed fever in a Jamaican jail, but Bonney disappeared from the record. Some historians believe that a relative bought her freedom and escorted her to Charleston or Virginia, where she lived out the rest of her days the luckiest woman alive.

Waccamaw Academy closed at the end of that school year spent playing cards, and we would be sent to the public elementary school in Socastee. My new public school took annual field trips to the pirate dungeon in the basement of the Old Exchange in Charleston, practically the epicenter of everything pirate-related. Melting wax figures of pirates chained to walls and pinned in torture forever between pieces of wood were displayed in its brick basement with the wide archways that looked like the bowing between the legs of cartoon cowboys. Another place of sorrow and haunted by all manner of ghosts. The pirates executed along with Stede Bonnet in the hanging purges that capped the Golden Age are said to scream and rattle their chains in the basement that is still called a dungeon. Hair is pulled, backs are pushed on stairwells, cold fingers are felt closing around throats.

Calico Jack was not the first or only pirate to fly a flag with fearsome images waving warnings to the ships and ports of the Carolinas. It was only his that caught on, for reasons lost, as he was not the most successful pirate, despite his progressive policies for aspiring lady pirates. The many flags of Black Bart show a sense of humor. A man in wide culottes standing on two skulls. A man in a tricorn hat toasting a skeleton. Blackbeard's flag depicted a devil throwing a spear at a red heart. A common school assignment was to draw and color a Jolly Roger of our own. Stacks of photocopied paper, blank but for the outline of a rectangle, sat at the corner of the teacher's desk for idle students to take and ponder the pirate life. In place of skull and crossbones, I layered wobbly circles and lines until my cat appeared.

My parents received a settlement from the trucking company, but it was not enough to cover their hospital bills and a new car, much less what was about to come. Dad could not wait tables for that first year after the wreck, and Mom began painting and wallpapering the homes of Nana's country-club friends for extra money. My parents did not hide their fighting from us, perhaps because it did not occur to them that we could hear their shouts. They considered us too young still to understand the implications of what they fought over, or maybe they considered us props in their own story, not yet writing our own. There was never enough money, and suggestions of selling the little brown house grew and grew. It was filled less and less with the love I knew.

8

Four of a Kind

IT WAS NOT THE RIGHT TIME FOR A NEW BABY, and so it was time for Mom to fall pregnant again. While Dad dreamed of country-music stardom, Mom had always wanted about a dozen kids, and Dad says now that he always felt the more, the merrier. Periodically, she'd ask me if I'd want a baby sister. Despite his assertions now, Jason claims that Dad was angry about the baby, before he came around. Mom was elated at first. She loved being pregnant, she says, but this time was different. The constant fighting, the anxiety over money and marriage, three children already, only a year apart each. In her fourth pregnancy, she did not swell with the ease and delight she expected. My memories of this pregnancy do not include Jason's, but are of Dad, without health insurance and back to waiting tables part-time, his leg not able to support his weight for long, limping with the gel-and-Velcro splint through Nana's house to collect us after work, and of Mom looking tired and holding her belly when she came one day to talk with my new teacher at the public school. My grades were always marked down for writing in lovely smooth cursive. "The other children haven't learned it yet" was the teacher's explanation.

Watching Westerns, Dad made lists of baby names on his legal pads from the blue paperback with the top-hatted storks on the cover. Shane or Luke. Mom wanted something starting with the letter J and thought it would be a girl, as she'd been sure I was going to be a boy. Summer air holds on to electricity, and maybe we were waiting on a crack of thunder that day at the end of July. My brothers and I were playing baseball in the front. Dad played guitar from the couch, and his whiskey-smoothed voice hovered over the bases. Mom had driven herself to the emergency room, but insisted that it was not an emergency. "You stay here and watch the kids," she urged Dad. And then to me, "Nicole, you stay here and watch over your dad." She's always doing that, begging us not to make a fuss over her, as if it's not habit after a lifetime. Recently she was bitten by a copperhead on the heel of her left foot, and it took her two days to get to a doctor. "It didn't seem so bad until it turned black," she said. I've had the thought to plant a ring of blackberry bushes around her house now, to attract black snakes that might eat the poisonous ones. What is the difference between that and Nana's hanging up that picture of Jesus with the Veronica Lake hair, or women who pour circles of salt around their homes as an act of protection? By the time she went to the hospital, it was too late for antivenom. Her foot remained a sight worth the pictures she sent for another two weeks until returning to its usual size and shape.

In the privacy of the emergency room of a Conway hospital—Lord knows what would have happened if she'd gone up to Myrtle Beach Hospital, a hospital where more than one Jones has gone for minor pains and been carried out dead—she relayed her symptoms. This man told her not to worry. Take some antibiotics, he scoffed, and he ignored the bulge of baby and her breath short from pain. He assumed she was sweating from the heat and not her already sky-high blood pressure. "Hot out today," he may have said, offering her a handkerchief. Then he wrote her a prescription to clear up an infection she didn't have. No big deal, really. Be gone by suppertime. I can hear his smugness, can feel his eagerness to be out of the room. So she came home still in pain and carrying a bag of fried chicken for my dad from Oliver's, just down the road from the hospital.

Her complexion hung gray against the blue, cloudless sky like the moon sometimes did during the daytime. We stopped playing and approached her, giving one another looks of worry. Dad heard the car door thump and came outside, a smile and cigarette hanging from his lips. I could tell just by the way he sucked in the air with his cigarette on the side. Mom's own lightness was vanishing, and when he saw, Dad strode forward with a purpose I rarely saw him possess. In his white tennis shorts and Drunken Jack's T-shirt, he looked just like my brother Justin, except for the shiny purple scar that crawled out of the splint from his ankle to his knee.

Dad moved the guitar from the couch and laid it on the coffee table, and it gonged as wood hit wood. The sound bounced around the room, not very loud, but silencing us all for a few seconds. Normally, he was so careful with the instrument and handled it more gingerly than he did his children. I heard it as an alarm, more than even the look of pain and worry on my mother's face. Dad called Nana from the rotary phone on the kitchen wall, the rubber of his shoes flapping on the parquet, a sound so normal and incongruous with the feeling in the air that I wished I hadn't heard it. I stood there in front of my brothers, staring at our mom, scared to move. She sat looking up through the skylights, bloated and waxy and near death with preeclampsia, though we didn't know it yet.

Not the most careful of drivers anyway, Nana sped inland toward our little brown house to reach her daughter-in-law, who I suspected she loved more than her son sometimes. Away from the beachfront villas of her neighbors. Down Highway 17. Through miles of pine trees. Turn down Highway 544. Over the turn-bridge and past the showboat that rested underneath. Then single trailers started to dot the side of the road. Locks of blond-white hair blowing with icy air-conditioning drafts. In her haste, she did not even bother to knot a scarf over her hair to keep it beauty-parlor perfect. She finally swished past the pampas grass that lined the streets of our neighborhood and pulled into the driveway.

The only other mother in the house, she got to work. She soaked a washcloth with cold water for Mom's forehead and told my father to get her to the hospital—again. Something is wrong, wrong, wrong. Often my dad and his brothers rolled their eyes at the advice of their mother. Though they protected her fiercely, Granddaddy's words had effected their damage, they had been conditioned slowly by their father's harshness to think of her as a woman with no sense. I watched as slowly, leaving our early childhood, my brothers and cousins talked down to Nana and clung more to one another, and excluded me from their games and business. We walked across King's Highway to splash around the pools and waves less and less, and they wandered in a pack of boys to convenience stores, to loiter in the parking lots of strip clubs in strip malls, like the Doll House right next to the Food Lion.

Together, Mom and Dad made their way to the white minivan that replaced the crumpled station wagon at a pace my mother's weakening state and expanded frame would allow for, wheels screeching with urgency as they pulled out of the driveway. A thud of bumper on concrete, and they were gone, just as they had been when they went to Nashville before the wreck. The house was quiet and unusually clean. My parents had not yet erected a crib or even decided where to put their fourth child, who was about to be born three months too soon.

Nana took us to her house, where she would have been expected, emergencies notwithstanding, to prepare a supper for Granddaddy, even if he didn't show up, and to watch over Chris and Brian. She often cooked something to try to ease our minds, which achieved the desired effect not with comforting and delicious food, but with our giggling at how badly she cooked. Her one want as a grandmother. Overcooked spaghetti topped only with Country Crock margarine. Cold hot dogs wrapped in a slice of Wonder Bread. Collards and butter beans that made the whole house stink like feet for days. The meanness of our glee did not occur to us, though we had surely picked it up from watching her husband and sons belittle her minor quirks so often they were verbally transformed into complete ineptitude. But the predictability of this routine was palliative. She would ask us what we wanted to eat, not if we were hungry.

Mom's condition should have correctly been diagnosed as preeclampsia when she went to the doctor that morning. She had to be airlifted to a town an hour and a half away and maybe there they could save her and the baby, but saving each or both was not a given. Florence, South Carolina, had been a minor hub in the regional railroad, and had transformed since its closing into a small town where there was a small highway junction and was thus full of truckers and the businesses that catered to them. Strangely, there was also a state-of-the-art neonatal hospital smack alongside the XXX video stores, the Burger Kings, and the road signs pointing you farther on to either the NASCAR racetrack in Darlington or the tourist strips of Myrtle Beach. My third brother was born at McCloud Regional Medical Center, which gleamed like a mirage, a miracle, in the middle of nowhere.

The calmest of my brothers was born the most violently almost three months early, and his middle name means "gift from God." Jared was born in emergency surgery, Mom sedated and nobody in the room to coo and cry over him. The doctors were more than half-surprised that he lived. For Dad, who trembled between gentleness and anger on normal days since the wreck, what could he have been thinking when the doctors could only say, "It's too soon to tell." He waited for days alongside his wife and his third son, the one who would look most like him, most like me. Jared weighed two pounds. He fit into the palm of an adult's hand and had not yet grown eyelashes and his skin that had yet to feel the light of day looked sunburned. Needles and IVs streamed from his tiny limbs and attached to a dozen machines that pumped him full of medicine and oxygen. A tube taped to his mouth ended in his lungs to breathe for him. His fingers and toes were translucent, the colors of Dad's scar when he first came home. I do not think I imagined watching the blood moving through his veins, the shadows of his organs.

For the weeks my mom was in the hospital, extending into the rest of the summer, my brothers and I stayed at Nana's house with our cousins. Nana's house was as good as home and where we stayed the last time there was an emergency with our parents, but then it was Dad who was hurt and Mom who came home. With our cousins, we splashed in the green slime of the pool, lit fires in the treehouse, or looked for money in Uncle Mike's couch. Nana reassured us that everything was okay, preferring to lie to us than to worry us, but I knew better. Dad stayed at the hospital with Mom, wearing only scrubs when his clothes became too dirty. Shuffling in sterile fabric that had to cover his hair, his feet, and his mouth, he visited her room and his son in the neonatal ward. Most of the babies, explained the nurses, were born to mothers who were drug addicts or were born dying. Dad called Nana's house to give updates on their conditions: Jared kept pulling the ventilator out of his lungs, and Mom was weak but awake.

One day in August, he creaked open the gate to Nana's backyard and walked up the sidewalk to her door. He moved slowly, slower than my grandparents, thin and hunched and wearing the sunglasses I'd last seen him in. A new cigarette swayed in his mouth, nodding up and down as he told us to get in the car. We played games the whole ride up, familiar with this stretch of highway from trips to Charlotte, and begged Dad to stop at the

fireworks stands on the side of the road. We knew that
we were getting close when we passed what could have
been a white-trash mirage of highway shopping in the
middle of the swamp where Francis Marion hid out so
long ago. Billboards of fading cartoon sombreros capped
the letters of the South of the Border signs that began to
crop up on roads that led to North Carolina. Fireworks
and gambling were not legal in that civilized northern
state, and the crumbling advertisements for what would
be contraband in a hundred miles were markers we
knew to look for. In this particular marker, there was a
boiled-peanut stand called Jimmy Carter Land, and his
squinting caricature looked down on the cars passing.
We didn't know Jimmy Carter as the former president.
To us, he was only the face welcoming us to the petting
zoo, fireworks outlet, doughnut shop, and a XXX video
store that also offered lacy lingerie.

Dad told us to be quiet and to behave once we got
to the hospital, but he didn't say much else. He seemed
changed already. For the first time, hints of a resem-
blance to his father peeked through his exhaustion. How
tiring to fight the nature that you don't care to claim.
Everything about the hospital seemed advanced, shiny,
and technological. That lives were saved here, you could
tell from the road. It felt not at all like the hospital in
Myrtle Beach. Dad told us not to touch her, just to hang
back on the sides and talk. She's been asking about you,
he said. I was not prepared for the relief of seeing her,
or for the way she looked, still bloated and gray. She lay

completely horizontal in the hospital bed, hooked up to the machines around her, and her voice was too soft to hear when she spoke. We stayed only a few minutes in her room, the blinds closed so she could rest. It was the only time I've seen her sleep without the television running in the background. Justin and Jason remembered Dad's instructions, but I hopped forward to touch her. My hand rested on hers briefly before, uncontrollably, I started to fall into a cramped hug. Dad grabbed my arm and whispered, "What did I tell you," in a hissing tone I had heard before, but not from him.

A nurse recognized Dad and waved us forward. She handed out sets of scrubs to me and to my brothers. For the first time, we would get to see Jared. I walked along the cracks of tiles to steady myself, despite years of mental drilling. Don't step on a crack. The refrain was a frivolous precaution at this point. Mom had already cracked open. Then there he was. Arms and legs squirming feebly among the wires. His chest rose and fell to the rhythm of the ventilator beside him. "He's strong," my dad murmured over and over. "Look how strong."

The nurse delivered Mom to us in a wheelchair, a sight more unnerving than that of her in the hospital bed. The day she was released from the hospital, my brothers stayed at Nana's house. The boys were too much to handle. She slept deeply and with the television playing in the background. I walked over and turned the set off, watching to see if the sudden absence of dialogue or the high pitch of static would wake her. Her physical fragility came through to me as I watched her sleep. I thought of her at home before Jared was born: skin pink and radiant and the heaviness of her pregnancy fixing her to the ground. It was a different kind of broken than the sadness I tried to prevent by following her around, no less permanent but still somehow more terrifying, after seeing her so close to vanishing permanently to a place where I would never find her. I watched her chest rise and fall and half expected her to float away.

I tiptoed out of her room and crossed the den to my bedroom, not knowing what to do with such a thought. I knew Dad would return from his cigarette run any second, but I climbed under the blankets on my bed, covering my whole self with their weight and lying in the comfort of darkness. As the knocking began and grew louder, I only wanted to hide. The doorbell started to sound, one ring on top of another, and I could tell he was angry. And suddenly, it stopped. I held my breath, hoping maybe he had gone away or that I might fall into sleep myself. That I would never be asked to do anything so big as be responsible for my mother again.

But then my door flew open. The sheets were ripped off the bed, clumsily they caught on his arms. What did I tell yous, mixed in the rustle of bedding. I felt Dad's hand, the one callused from guitar strings, on my head. For a second, it was the same motion as his patting the top of our collie's head, but then his fingers laced through my hair and pulled. In this way, he pulled me off the bed and onto the floor. Never losing his grip, a good one

right at the scalp, he dragged me through the door frame
and into the den. My heels and my thighs burned from
the friction as I moved across the rug. Twisting around,
I saw my mother half naked and leaning against a wall,
too weak to come any farther. She had answered the
door in my place and now watched him struggle with
himself.

He had tried so hard all his life to be better than
the father who beat him senseless. He was the one who
followed his mother around, willing protection on her
through the power of his presence alone, and when that
didn't work, he grew up and fought back. I didn't want
to fight back. Consumed with grief and tired to the soul,
Dad couldn't help but fall into the ease of the oldest pattern he knew. Was this was what it meant to be a Jones?
He seemed to find himself just in time, and he let me go
with soothing sorrys and songs all afternoon. Though
I'm sure I was mad, even then I realized that I knew him
better for it. We were now more alike than he'd wanted
us to be, and as he had done, too, I found solace as well
as adventure and opportunity in putting words on paper. He had stopped singing like he used to after the
wreck, but once Jared came home, after two months in
the neonatal hospital, softly at first and then almost like
his old self, Dad sang to his third son to the beeping
metronome of the rented heart monitor and whirr of the
oxygen tank. Just like Nana sang to us and to himself,
"You Are My Sunshine."

There is an alley in Charleston between Church

and State Streets called officially Philadelphia Alley but known to most as Dueler's Alley, where duels were held under the law until the 1880s. The walls are high and of red brick. Trees grow leggy to reach the sun and planters filled with tropical ferns and neon azalea line its narrowness. It connected to a graveyard, though that is no feat in a city as old as Charleston. Here went the honorable drunken men, gentle or not, to resolve their rows with pistols at dawn. Here we find the ghost of a young doctor among all the rest. A man from Rhode Island, Dr. Ladd, found room and board at the yellow house with the green shutters on Church Street, and so happy was Dr. Ladd here that Charlestonians knew him by his whistling. A friend became jealous of his popularity, and after a prolonged falling-out over things lost to time, challenged Dr. Ladd to a duel. He was shot in Dueler's Alley, where translucent men and gunshots are oft heard, but died in the house on Church Street. For centuries since, Charlestonians have caught the ghost of Dr. Ladd whistling up and down Church Street, and in the darkness of Dueler's Alley. The constant humming of Dad over Jared's crib remind me of Dr. Ladd's soft whistles, content-sounding but also eerie, not quite right. He wasn't reachable is what it was.

Before Jared was a year old, my parents had to sell the little brown house in Conway to pay down the medical bills. There was no room for us at Nana's house, already home to Uncle Mike and his sons. Grandpa let us move into a beach cottage he owned in Cherry Grove, on the north end of the Low Country. On our first night in Cherry Grove, Justin, Jason, and I followed an illuminated lane of mid-summer moonlight to the wooden steps leading down to the beach. It's a strange patch of elevated Low Country, right next to the pier, in a region known for the appearance of straightforward flatness. Usually, even the outstretched arms of high tide stayed yards beyond the stairs, a sunbather's sandy dream. That night, some unseen storm of low pressure beyond the horizon was met by the full moon's arms so that the water and its waves swelled to storm-surge heights. We were drawn to the cusp of that veiled realm, as children in books are unable to resist forbidden forests and beckoning songs their parents cannot detect. It was a calm, clear night otherwise, but we knew our beaches intimately as beach kids do and could tell the greedy undulation of our normally placid water was not for swimming. We sat on the very top step practically still on North Ocean Boulevard, that's how high the ocean reached, and we held tight to the wooden railing as warm water lifted our little brown bodies with the ease of wind tugging a feather. We giggled and screamed as the summer sea licked at our arms and faces and sucked at our toes, pulling at our whole selves as magnets pulled. We were giddy with feeling the power of what lay unseen and unsaid on our skin. Such a force was nearly singing with joy in a language I could not quite make out, and I imagined all the maidens and sailors ever lost at sea had thrown an underwater ball. This was not an angry sea, but one stretching for the pleasure of its own power like a cat upon waking. This was not the night for blood sacrifices, and as children are creatures connected by imagination to the unknown, we were blessed with a show just for us.

Soaking wet, we laughed our way across the boulevard, to the screened-in porch where Dad smoked and sang. I recall jangly songs of vacation and escape in place of the country choruses. He'd put his own music down for the longest period I'd seen him in the three years between the wreck and Jared's birth, questioning whether it was even worth it to try any longer. The guitar remained in its case in a closet. Together on the porch, he taught us the words to Beach Boys songs about other beachy islands. We never harmonized as well as he tried to teach us, but we defied gravity in our own way that first night. This is the point in the story before our characters make a decision, for good or for bad, the dreamy hit of nicotine inhaled and held inside before breathing out things you can't take back once released. It was this summer in Cherry Grove that I disappeared a little more fully into the sanctuary of imagination that springs from the space between pages, where I visited stories for their safety, their reliability, as I saw Nana escape into the sanctuary of her books.

I was taught in history class about Theodosia Burr, the placidly beautiful daughter of Aaron Burr who was lost at sea during a storm off Cape Hatteras. That, at least, is the commonsense theory, though she and her ship may well have been captured by pirates, and the passengers forced to walk the plank. Some say she's been walking the shore a few counties up, looking for her treasure, which was also given to the ocean. Brookgreen Gardens tries to claim her ghost, saying she walks among the statues near her husband's grave, but I don't buy it. Perhaps I shied away from Theodosia because embedded in stories about her tragic death was the subtle spin that she brought it on herself, the same as Alice did. Are the legends of her mysterious fate imposed on her as some sort of punishment? She was one of the few educated women of her time. Her father, before gunning down Alexander Hamilton, figured Theodosia worthy of schooling, and she was the first educated woman I had heard of. A New Yorker, no less, who was still deemed worthy of a Southern ghost story. In a townhouse in Greenwich Village, she read her Greek and hosted parties and married a man, the future governor of South Carolina, who valued her knowledge at least as much as any other offerings of marriage. Was it the ocean taking revenge on an unnaturally educated woman when it pulled her and her ship down? More likely the kneading of history by men. This is what happened to women who didn't know their place. Who had a fancy New York education and thought themselves as valuable as their husbands, and who let them know it, to boot. They walked the plank and were eaten alive by sharks in the cold dark sea. If pirates managed to overtake her ship, I like to think of either Anne Bonney or Mary Read stepping on board to loot and pillage, recognizing Theodosia as another mouthy, ambitious woman and hitting it off. I could feel the crystals of salt clinging to my tangled and windswept hair, the metal of a dagger cool as rain strapped to my ankle, and the weight of a blade on my hip. How close the sour tang of marsh air. The fire-crackle snaps of thousands of pistol shrimp in the mud as the flames of sunrise seep from horizon into land. Maybe we could all take tea together before sailing off to an imagined land where their dispositions were not punishable, by noose or plank.

Sometimes Dad took me to the Cherry Grove pier to fish or to the beach for rounds of catch with baseballs sometimes landing in the waves. For hours, we'd throw back and forth until his instructions fell into silence. It was an uneasy time for all of us, and I remember very little of Mom then. Perhaps she was busy taking care of Jared, who turned a year old that summer. As I was nine when he was born, I feel half his sibling and half his guardian. I remember feeding him and the foul smell of formula, rocking him to sleep, holding up his fat wrists as he took first steps. I was the oldest and only girl. The boys were not going to be asked to babysit, I knew by then. They were as free to roam and loiter as they always were, bringing home sunburned shoulders and hermit crabs collected on the beach or bought at a strip mall. Jared rode my own kid-narrow hips as much as Mom's. Through the bond of attention or the gamble of genes, he has grown up the most like me, and the good folks of

South Carolina, well-meaning, have asked if we are not identical twins.

He was a good baby, his teeth the only sign of the months he spent in the hospital instead of our home. They came in rotted away through the middle in tiny arches and sharp as razor blades on their ends. The older boys and I thought it was funny to teach him to bite the others, until our own blood was drawn. I remember him crying only once. Mom had been crying about something I could feel and nothing she'd say, after driving around with me and Jared, driving home from Nana's perhaps. She pulled into the parking lot of Belk, the local department store, and said she'd be back in a minute. Of course, I whined for her not to go, it was dark and late and, in my memory, pouring rain. After a few minutes turned into ten and then twenty and more, Jared shrieked inconsolably. His screams, so loud from such a tiny thing, burned in the darkness, squalls pounded our minivan, and suddenly I was begging God and Jesus above to please help. I did not know what to do. Wrapped inside the veil of wan streetlight, I thought of the night she hit a deer with our old station wagon. A memory forgotten on purpose or hiding with the other creatures that came out only at night. We had been driving back from a visit to Grandpa's house. The boys slept, and I lay awake watching the stars skip over tree branches. The webworms waved and beckoned. Car headlights floated into our den and then flickered gone. Mom hummed or sang softly with the radio. The sounds of the drive rose

and fell alongside the chests of my sleeping brothers, between the slow blinks. I was never a good sleeper. Still
I hesitate to close eyes in need of rest, reluctant to miss
what entity might lurk between imagination and presence. The lurching thud and invisible hands pulling me
backward even as I shot forward, like on a roller coaster,
and suddenly we are at a gas station. Mom is sobbing
under the same sickly gray yellow as the parking-lot
lights at the mall, and a gas station attendant, an old
skinny man in a dirty uniform, is examining the front of
the car where she hit a deer.

Finally, Mom came back out with a small plastic
bag. Anger and relief welled up in tangles, and I could
say nothing. Jared quieted with her return, a mother's
presence one of the few things I couldn't give him. Now
I see clearly a need for the luxury of five minutes to herself, away from a depressed husband on the edge of ad-
diction, and four kids, one needier than the next. Just
to be alone, to breathe without small hands grasping at
her legs or breasts. To contemplate something new for
herself from all the unused things around her, and then
the need to have something to look forward to, an object through which to imagine herself anew. In silence,
tears surged and splashed. They fell from her, and they
fell from me. Every salty drop connected me to her and
her to me like the shining links of filigree that Nana had
given to her, that she would one day give to me. Perhaps
Jared could sense not just the storm outside, but a temptation flaring, even for just a second, hot and dry in the

clammy rain. She could leave us all as her own mother had done and be free of all this, but she just started up the car.

Nana had once attempted to claim her freedom and had tried to get out of Myrtle Beach. She rocked in her recliner and looked at me on the couch when she told me about packing a bag and taking off. Granddaddy's waitress F had been coming around more and more, and all the boys were grown and out of school. She got in the car and was driving up to Columbia to stay with her friend Joree. When she got to Florence, an hour outside of Myrtle Beach, she saw flashing lights in the rearview window. "Can I help you, Officer? I don't know what I was doin' wrong." She had only been a pretty blonde he'd wanted to talk to until he saw the last name on her driver's license. The Joneses had the lawmen in their pockets, they bragged.

"What are you doin' so far from home, Mrs. Jones?"

"Sir, I'm leaving my husband."

"No, you're not. You're going back home."

Back in the present, her voice unwavering and matter-of-fact, "He followed me all the way back to the driveway too."

She wanted me to know that she had tried to leave. That she had wanted to. That not everybody gets to move freely in the world. That is what she wanted for me.

9

Whiskey Jones

GRANDDADDY HAD BEEN TELLING DAD TO GIVE up on music for years.

"I just don't see how on earth you gonna make a living is all," he said in his office at the Sandcastle. It was a gentle tack for him. "You gotta be thinking about them kids, Mark. You don't have time for none of this guitar nonsense."

He meant as well as he ever had. Better, I suppose, as even he could see that Dad was in a bad spot. His leg was holding up better than the rest of him. Granddaddy had a philosophy of not helping anybody but himself, and even in my dad's broken state, he would never give him a job or lend him a dime. Perhaps unused to compassionate tones from Granddaddy or too tired to imagine anything anymore, Dad decided to open his own restaurant. He'd managed his uncle Herman's Pancake House in Garden City for years. Another Jones getting into the restaurant business, feeding tourists. It was the way of things.

Love needs something to look forward to, and my parents needed something new that did not come with an outstanding balance in a number-ten envelope. They did not need to look too far. Like anybody who really knows how to make a buck, like Granddaddy and Uncle Jack, their brother Herman seemed willing to overlook irregularities of the financial kind if it meant he could take advantage of collecting later. According to family stories, anyway. Like his brothers, he hit his bottom line and seemed to care little about at whose expense, and he rented to my parents an empty two-story building in an orange stucco finish with white columns out front at the end of a strip mall on King's Highway, a few blocks down from Captain Hook's Pirate Adventure Mini-Golf in one direction and Nana's house in the other. The front door opened onto black-and-white checkered tile that led back to the wide oak bar with a mirror taking up the wall behind it, where I'd watch myself do homework in the afternoon all during middle school. To the right was an open space in front of a real, if small, stage that Dad built. A place to perform his music whenever he wanted to. Ronnie Milsap had opened the Carolina Opry, Dolly Parton had a new dinner theater on Restaurant Row, the Dixie Stampede, an extravaganza of incorrect history on

horseback. Nashville might come to him. He saw himself as part old-fashioned bartender, part sheriff, like in
the Westerns he grew up with. The type of bar owner
who could shoot the breeze with the regulars and just
plain shoot the troublemakers. Who could entertain a
crowd. Who wore shiny vests and bolo ties and sleeve
garters. Maybe a costume would have improved some
decisions. If you dress up to perform, maybe it is easier
to remember who you are once you take it off. We'd have
teased him for it, anyway, so it is probably best he kept
to T-shirts and ball caps.

Dad's initial excitement for anything new was infec-
tious, and Mom kept right along, handing Jared, now
toddling around off the oxygen tank, over to me to watch
while she cleaned the whole place from top to bottom,
picking out silverware and painting the walls. "What
should we call the place?" Dad asked this of us on every
car ride home once we started fixing the place up. My
brothers and I would shout out names all at once, silly
ones like the names given to the vacation beach houses
on Ocean Boulevard. The Saloon. Dad's Place. The Hurricane Hole. The Jukebox. The game shortened the car
ride home, an hour or more up to Cherry Grove, inching
along Restaurant Row in summertime traffic, passing
more of Uncle Herman's Calabash restaurants, like the
one with the giant crab erected around its front door.

Whispers from the muses, ancestors dead and gone,
or else buried psychology. "Whiskey Jones," Dad said
one day in the parking lot. He said it louder once again

and smiled, unaware of a moment I look back on as fore-
shadowing, though I'd still wear the T-shirt. The logo
really was something. Not quite Drunken Jack's, but
a man who could have passed for a brother in a pan-
ama hat, linen suit, and glasses. The sign has long been
locked up in a storage unit of Uncle Herman's, taken as
collateral for rent unpaid, so I cannot confirm the mon-
ocle, but let's throw it in for fun.

For a minute, it was the hottest place in Myrtle
Beach, but it's hard to keep up the effort of service when
your heart's not in it. It's hard to break even when you're
giving the drinks away, and it gets harder still to notice
you're short-changing yourself when you're knocking
back your own drinks. Having accepted his fate as any
other Jones of Myrtle Beach, just one more son of sons
in the restaurant business, resignation filled up the cups
but not the bank. As if that wasn't enough, they'd found
one bank that loaned them a down payment for a new
house in Little River, just inland from Cherry Grove,
over a different swing bridge that we had to cross every
day to get to school. We were often late, when the bridge,
with limbs like a daddy longlegs, twisted away from the
main road, looking as if it were dangling the spidery legs
over the Intracoastal Waterway, so that tall fishing boats
and barges could float through the narrow passage. Our
new house, a big blue one, was too perfect-looking for us
and our perilous finances, which still included a mountain of medical debt from keeping Jared and Mom alive,
two years after he came home from the hospital. There

are priceless things, but life has never been one of them. Their medical debt came to hundreds of thousands. The big blue house in Little River had a wraparound porch, but it would never be the little brown house in Conway.

We drove up and down King's Highway in Mom's new minivan, a Christmas gift from Grandpa the year we were living at the beach house. It seemed like a modern marvel, with sliding doors on both sides and painted a deep galactic green. Like our big blue house, it felt like it didn't match our family's state. Beaten down by one bad break after another, surviving as always due to the generosity of family until it was too much effort to imagine escaping. My strongest memory of the alien green minivan is that we could not afford to fix the things that went wrong with it. The windshield stayed cracked. The sliding doors stopped opening. The wipers broke and had to stay that way for weeks. On the drive to Nana's house for Christmas one year, rain and sleet fell in obscuring coats across the windshield already black with night. All the restaurant lights and signs for seafood were unlit for the holiday. Mom pulled over on some roadside grass before getting to the swing bridge, tears of anger falling down her cheeks in flat lines through the shimmer of her face powder. She twisted around from the driver's seat in total silence, the only true tell of her mood, and pulled a large dinosaur toy from Jared's hands. Rolling down her window, she curled her arm around the front so she could wedge the long plastic tail on the *Tyrannosaurus rex* into the closer wiper blade, and moving

the dinosaur, gripped by the neck, up and down with
the window wide open to the freezing rain, that is how
we traveled the hour to Nana's house. Soaked but safe.
How sore her arm must have been. For a while during
these years, I became more afraid of space aliens than
of ghosts, and made Mom sit on the edge of the bathroom sink while I showered. Sometimes, after pushing
back the shower curtain with a clanging of rusty hooks,
I'd emerge to find she had quietly left me there alone,
and the heartbeat of panic recalled the night in the mall
parking lot when I thought she might leave, when I realized that she could.

Most afternoons during the school year, we were
ferried down to Whiskey Jones with backpacks full of
homework and a list of chores to complete before the
doors opened for happy hour. It was always tight. I
would put my bag down on the checkered tile and head
behind the bar, stained dark and glazed with finisher
and the foggy tracings of spilled drinks. The bar, ba-
roque and heavy, stretched the length of the front room
and held up a wide mirror that doubled it. My everyday
jobs were to cut the oranges, limes, and lemons for the
drinks, arrange them in orange, green, and yellow hol-
lows of the plastic white trays. Even now the smell of
limes reminds me of being behind the bar, barely able
to see over the top, feet squishing on and sticking into
the black rubber anti-fatigue mat, slicing them first into
half-moons and then waning wedges with the slits in the
middle for easy sliding onto the rims of glasses. Often I

put Jared to bed at night when my parents worked, and I'd repeat, not quite singing, but in sing-song whispers, "I see the moon and the moon sees me. God bless the moon and God bless me," until his laughs and repetitions turned to snores.

Cleaning up the bar most afternoons after school, I turned the glasses smeared with fingerprints and lipstick upside down and stuck them onto the black bristles shaped like fir trees in the sink. When my tasks were done, I settled down at the bar and watched myself write homework in the mirror, continuing even when the first patrons trickled in, then my brothers and I walked to Nana's house to spend the evening. In the dimmed lights, surrounded by the dark stained wood of the bar, the shadows under the dozens of round tables in front of the stage, it felt as if a storm were always in the air, echoes of our parents' arguments. I expected the clouds Mom painted on the wall, drawn in pencil above the Low Country marsh by Dad's friend Clay, a silhouette artist, to light the dark, empty dining room with bouts of lightning, to flood the dining room with rain.

Along each edge of the bar's mirror, a waxy wood mermaid was carved naked at the waist but for tendrils of waving hair, her arms overhead to look as if she were holding aloft the top beam that connected the mirror to the ceiling. At my middle school, North Myrtle Beach Middle School, I had learned about the Mermaid Riots in Charleston. After weeks or months of confounding daily downpours that refused to clear by prayers to Jesus, a young doctor was accused of keeping captive a mermaid. This had angered the spirits that ruled the sea, it was clear. The good Christians of eighteenth-century Charleston thus gathered in a mob of top-hatted gentlemen swimming through the streets and rowboats containing any ladies who dared, and few churchgoing Southern ladies could resist the chance to run someone out of town. Regrettably, no torch kept alight in the heavy rain, but there were pitchforks and muskets to go around. And so this congregation of Charlestonians, probably all resting now in the tourist-filled graveyards of the Holy City, pounded on this doctor's front door, demanding that he release the mermaid he held captive for the selfish sacrilege of science. It should go without saying that this guy was "from off." The doctor was carried through the flooded streets toward the Battery, the seaside promenade that barricades Rainbow Row from the harbor, with the mermaid swimming in a glass jar, where he dumped her back into the ocean. Hallelujah, the rain stopped, say the books, which propose that this mermaid was nothing more than an unusually large frog or a baby manatee. If these ancestors of mine, Low Country people since before the days of Francis Marion, couldn't tell the difference between a mythical sea creature and a garden frog, I might rather be descended from the frog. That the good doctor most likely kept a baby manatee was not very hard to figure out. The broad, slow rolls of their gray-brown bulk are still seen lolling in the rivers and marsh creeks every summer. Sailors had been mistaking their good-natured surface sunning for the enticement of mermaids since the Spanish landed in Georgetown.

Sometimes I wondered what would happen if I severed one of these mythic idols from her perch above the bar and offered it up on my own to the ocean. I could easily slip away and walk across King's Highway through the elephant-tall dunes onto the beach, and it would probably not be that hard to get hold of a crowbar or hatchet. Would some relief come for my parents, for the floods of tears my mom cried, if I gave to the sea the only mermaid I had access to? Would the safety of music return and their worry stop falling as the rain in Charleston had ceased? Such an offering might make me as bad as the men who spread such a ridiculous tale. I would be participating, acquiescing to a world built on the ill-formed stories and logic of men that did not feel true to me. If I was going to get into the business of telling ghost stories, I might get to change the endings.

I never took an ax to the figureheads that watched my parents disintegrate into their worst selves. Instead, after our chores on most days, we'd walk to Nana's house to finish our homework and either spend the night there with Chris and Brian, or wait for Mom to pick us up around midnight. Dad always stayed till closing, but he'd do more than just lock the doors. After the excitement of finding a venue with a stage and hosting a few gigs at the beginning, he let that vital part of him fall away, and the stage was dark and empty for most of our time at Whiskey Jones. An entertainer without a stage, he soon found a crowd of regulars to keep him company as they took advantage of my dad's proximity to the alcohol and the cash registers. They were similarly good-humored men, for the most part, with dead-end jobs and no goals beyond a good time, who would dull the pain of being stuck in a small town, in a small life, with drinks and cocaine. Soon my dad followed suit.

He'd get home just as the sun was coming up, drunk enough to fall asleep with the car door open and one leg on the gravel. Mom would wait up for him, and just like in all the songs, would ask him where he'd been all night, even though she knew. It's one of those tunes that gets in your head and just won't stop playing. What would start as angry muffled voices became explosive, slurred screams. I knew he had passed out in the front seat if I heard the car come up the driveway, but not the bang of the front door slamming. I knew my brothers heard it, too, and at least if they were fighting, Dad was home.

Eventually he started sleeping all the way in the car, when he came home at all, and the only chorus we heard was Mom singing for a change. "Get out of my house" will probably not make the Top Ten anytime soon. I'd wake up for school and look out the window first thing. Some days, Mom wouldn't come out of her room if Dad was there. She told us through the locked door to have him take us to school. So my brothers and I would shuffle out to the car and knock on the window. Dad would creak to life and mumble for us to get in. He'd drive us the ten minutes to North Myrtle Beach Middle School, not saying anything and probably still drunk. One morning, Justin was climbing into the front passenger seat, and Dad started backing up, reversing fast. Justin was knocked flat, but at least not run over.

Like Mom, I hated his new friends. The artists and musicians he'd known since childhood were replaced by the goalless and grungy. The magician who ogled my eleven-twelve-thirteen-year-old body when I was working at the bar. Dad claims that he saw the magician bend a spoon backward with his mind and that he made Uncle Herman cry, a feat no man had been known to do, with a trick he did for tips at the bar.

"Hey, man," said my dad to the magician. "Herman just walked in, and I ain't got the rent. Do something to distract him."

The magician approached my great-uncle, who, like my granddaddy, his younger brother, did not then keep animals. "Think of the name of your favorite pet, and I will write it down." He scrawled a few letters on a square white napkin, soggy from the condensation of free drinks my dad doled out, and slid it over to Herman, who then sobbed like a baby. "Red was the name of the only dog I ever loved." I remember no magic on the part of this magician. Only eyes that clung, which I was long familiar with. Not just from pageants, but as any girl is by then. The jokes about chastity belts to parents who laughed politely and the close-up leers of patrons I was not as used to putting up with in quiet politeness. The urge to stab my paring knife into the hand of the magician every time it slid across the bar in my direction I grew used to managing and smiling through. I had been prepared my whole life to deflect with magnanimity the repulsions and violent urges induced by unwanted advances. Less conspicuous was more safe.

If the wreck hastened a giving-up for my parents, then the restaurant would be the giving-in. This was the place where their individual failures and disappointments would break their marriage. There was no hope for us after the restaurant. They would not officially divorce for three more messy years, but the writing was on the wall Mom had so lovingly painted. My brothers and I were waiting for it. Like the relief of four o'clock rain in summer. When Dad finally sat us down in the living room of a new house in a new town and gave us the usual lines from country songs, we knew the words by heart. Children see everything, even the ghosts and creatures adults have long shoved under the bed. As my dad, his words and his presence echoed with truth and authority. He was the biggest star there was in my eyes, which were not the stage he needed. These are dark and drug-hazy times, and it's bad manners to linger, so let us turn the page, as it is in our power to do here, when it so often in life is not. The mercy of time and the whims of the weather. A counterclockwise wind is gusting.

10

Hurricane Games

As rules are kept to by the real and respectable ghosts of the Low Country, here follow the
rules for hurricanes:

> One: 74 to 95 miles per hour. "Very danger-
> ous winds will produce some damage."
> Two: 96 to 110 m.p.h. "Extremely dangerous
> winds will cause extensive damage."
> Three: 111 to 129 m.p.h. "Devastating dam-
> age will occur."
> Four: 130 to 156 m.p.h. "Catastrophic dam-
> age will occur."
> Five: 157 m.p.h. or higher. "Catastrophic
> damage will occur."

Surely the good gentlemen of the National Oceanic and Atmospheric Administration did not lack a thesaurus. If such a repetition were in a song, I would say that such a choice must have been made to invoke a rhythm, to emphasize an outcome, to imbed a theme. But then I think, well, there is no point in nuance once you get to catastrophe. The scale is a tool for alerting people in the way of what to go about saving, or the people watching on far-off TVs how much popcorn to make. It does not count rainfall, tornados, storm surge, and wind gusts. It is only the sustained winds that are tallied above. The formation of a hurricane is the next step for a tropical storm, which originates with what they call a tropical depression. Nature gets the blues, like the rest of us, I suppose, and only tearing something up helps. I cannot blame the weather for something I am guilty of myself.

Hazel, which arrived in 1954, is credited with transforming Myrtle Beach into the family-friendly and affordable tourist destination that it is today. Out to sea washed the beachfront shacks and up went the roadside motels, largely built by the H. C. Jones Construction Company. Aerial photographs of the area after storms are popular as postcards and on book-jacket covers of souvenir histories. Where lumber and bricks upheld dreams and protected a family of memories, there stood empty lots or piles of broken beams and debris. The pictures of Hazel seem to always be sold in a wash of sepia brown. Tourists buy prints of other people's catastrophe, marveling at the unimaginable. I hope these are talismans by which they count their blessings, but I have a feeling that they are just turning a natural disaster into an attraction. At least the Pavilion did not wash away. No, that marvel was destroyed by nothing so marvelous in scale as a hurricane. Only the everyday greed of shortsighted men.

The summer my parents announced their first separation in what would be a long series of rifts and reconciliations was a particularly active hurricane season for our stretch of South Carolina coast. At the very least, I will remember the blue house in Little River that was the scene of so much fighting and unhappiness as having the best front porch of all the houses we lived in. Mom spent days searching secondhand stores for rocking chairs to fill the porch and then painting them white to match the railings. Maybe she thought their wide arms would hold her family together. Not long after we moved in, even our beloved Bandit died. Mom picked us up from Nana's after midnight, and as my brothers squirmed unseatbelted between bites of fast food in the green van, she began to cry in thin creaks at first and then sobs; unusual, as her angry tears were always quiet. Along the familiar neon stretch of Restaurant Row and past Briarcliffe Mall across the street from the Meher Baba ashram we didn't know was there, she got it out that Bandit wouldn't be coming home with us. His heart was infected with parasites, and they could only afford to put him down instead of treat him. Not long after, she said to us in the car, "We're shutting down the restaurant."

"We know," said her three eldest kids in unison. We knew it all, of course. They hadn't been able to pay the rent for months, and Uncle Herman, a teetotaler like Granddaddy, would take the sign and whatever else he could sell in the building. The bank was about to take the house, and we were officially moving to Charlotte.

Little River was one of Blackbeard's hideouts. He buried treasure all over the inlets in our neighborhood. Glittering jewels and doubloons sparkling in the swamps and mud-colored waterways. The man who finally killed Blackbeard, Robert Maynard, was hired by the governor of Virginia to track down the most fearsome pirate of the Golden Age of Piracy. Maynard sent spies in canoes up waterways like the one by our new house to discover where the pirate and his crew were hiding. In a battle off Ocracoke Island, Blackbeard was captured and killed, his head displayed from the mast of Maynard's ship and his body thrown overboard. The legends say that it swam headless in laps around the ship before sinking to the bottom of the ocean. My brothers and I roamed the neighborhood and the banks of the water with sticks and Super Soaker water guns, pretending to be pirates ourselves. We had been waiting and watching our parents take out their unhappiness on each other, and we wondered what was going to happen in the safety of the sappy pine lots, tracking the course of their love like we tracked the hurricanes swooshing across the Atlantic during the fall. In fact, before Hugo blew into town years before, the biggest news from our coast had been the discovery of a shipwreck that yielded one of the largest hauls of gold ever found on the bottom of the ocean, pulled up from the *Central America*, which had gone down in 1857.

It was only a few weeks after my early-June birthday when the first storm of the season danced past our home, whisking over the whitecaps beyond the local pier and skimming the Outer Banks to the north of us. A sharp elbow to the gut of the Atlantic, awkwardly bumping into the faceless names that crowd the ocean floor. A for Arthur. Though technically within the bounds of the season, a hurricane in June was unusual enough to feel like an omen. I had cut out the hurricane chart the paper published every year on June 1, the first official day of hurricane season, and tacked it on the wall, as I did every year. I usually didn't have to start marking latitudes and longitudes until the end of August. We often did it as a class assignment in the first weeks of a new school year, watching as our little crisscross marks of ink or colored pencil curved out from the bubble of western Africa. Hurricanes were tricksters, moody spirits, and just about the only thing you could count on was their changing course at the last minute. X marks the spot, we'd note on our tracking charts, where the eye came ashore, penciling its path from a school desk till the name disappeared, usually around Canada somewhere, under my name in the top right corner of the page. If the X fell close to us, we'd be at home on a hurricane day, unless it was a category four or five, and even then it depended.

Most locals don't feel like following the blue hurricane evacuation signs out of town, and storms like Hugo and Hazel were once-a-generation-type storms. Besides, it was harder to return than it was to leave. When you're desperate to know if your house is still standing, the National Guard blocking the highway back to the only home you've known is not a sight to imbue patience in a population prone to temper.

B for Bertha. I pretended to be asleep one morning about a month after Arthur, lying in my parents' bed, Mom's at that point, and listening to the Weather Channel. Mom slept with the TV on, when she slept at all, and I heard the hurricane watch issued for our county as I tried not to move. Meteorologists showed pictures of churning waters, and red warning flags flapped and seized against gray skies. They seemed excited. I was excited, too. I loved a good storm, and hurricanes were the best storms of all. As it was summer vacation, Bertha wouldn't get us a day off school, but it was still something to look forward to. In a thunderstorm, you could feel the electricity in the air. The rumble of thunder. The crackle of lightning. Voluminous clouds that morphed and swirled messages from unknowable worlds, changing colors as fast as a mood ring. The power of it made my bones hum. I had never lost anything or anybody in a hurricane before, as generations past were so used to. Even families who had lost everything to wind and water—either loved ones or beloved home—remained stoic in the face of other storms. In a recent storm, a friend joked that he had left all his unwanted junk on the porch and the storm better blow it all away, 'cause he was so sick of looking at it.

Dad came home one day with sheets of plywood, masking tape, and coils of rope. We had a day before Bertha would come ashore, in Little River, projected the men on TV. Mom stayed in bed with Jared, following the weather reports and avoiding my dad. When I got up from the bed, she asked me to close the door. Downstairs, Dad had rounded up Justin and Jason and started giving them instructions. Tie the bicycles in the backyard to the back porch so they don't blow away. Clear the yard of Jared's toys so they don't blow away. Pick up fallen branches and fishing poles or anything else that looked like it might blow away and throw them in the pond in the woods out back. I taped big Xs on all the windows of the house, so the glass wouldn't shatter if it was hit by toys forgotten in the grass or tree limbs flying through the air. When the official warning came down the day of, Little River was just on the south edge of the danger zone, the last county shaded red on the map, as the eye had shifted toward Wilmington. The Gray Man rested unseen, so there was nothing to worry about anyway. Mom had gone to the store for candles, matches, water, batteries, and other things we had requested in case we were without power and cable television for several days. Junk food and an extra pack of cards. Dad went to fill up on gas. They did everything separately except fight, and I was the most nervous when they said nothing to each other. It was almost but not quite like the air of Nana's house when Granddaddy was home. Everybody knows that a reprieve from the winds too soon means the worst of the storm can return at any moment. The eye of the storm was always as quiet as our blue house.

The day before Bertha was scheduled to come ashore, we all went to the beach. It is a tradition to go to the beach before a hurricane. We watched the waves grow fat and swollen and happy with what was to come. Surfers came to the beach before storms for this reason. The surf was normally too calm to ride, and a storm offshore meant better waves to catch. The feathery grass that covered the sand dunes twitched where it normally waved in slow sighs. Stores and restaurants had messages spray-painted on plywood covering their windows: GO HOME BIG BERTHA and BERTHA YOU COW. The winds were beginning to pick up, though just from looking at the sky, it looked like a perfect summer day. I remembered stories of bodies blown and washed into the branches of oak trees next to dangling and angry snakes, Medusa's head come to life, though I may have read this in a book somewhere.

We went from the beach to Nana's house, where she told, as she always would before a storm threatened, the story of her biggest hurricane loss. She told this story before every tease or thrill of tropical weather, returning to the days after Hurricane Hazel from her rocking recliner with the view of the patio and magnolia tree.

"My mama went through a nervous breakdown when she went through menopause, according to the doctors, so her family sent her down to a hospital in Charleston. I don't think they do the shock treatment anymore, do they?" she asked me every time, long before I knew what shock treatment or menopause was, and so I said nothing and listened, as Dad paced on the patio with a cigarette and one or more of his brothers. Mom and my brothers and cousins were out of sight.

"Well, her people were all from Florida originally, so when she got done in the hospital, she took the train from Florence to Florida. That was the night Hurricane Hazel hit. We didn't know in advance in those days. My daddy was so upset. He was walkin' between my sister Sue's and my houses. We only lived a street away from each other, until finally we took the kids—your daddy wasn't born yet—and we went down to the church to wait. He said, 'It's a sad thing when it takes a hurricane to get you in church.' We'd all gone to the church basement that night." She could have told the story about her neighbor's call to warn her of Hazel's approach, and their flight door-to-door to warn as many people as they could. It was a story she told every time we drove past Thirty-third Avenue, no matter the season. Never had she connected the stories, and what was lost for my not noticing until now?

"The day Mama got back two weeks later, he had died in his sleep at about five o'clock that morning." Still I sat silently, not knowing how to acknowledge the weight of her loss. She said to me, as she often did, "I bet you're tired of hearing me talk."

"Nana, that's why I ask, to listen to you talk," I said.

A lifetime of Granddaddy telling her to shut her mouth, telling us how stupid she was, had left her self-conscious of her stories. I grew hungrier to hear her voice as I got farther away from her. I regret to say that medical care for women in the South has little improved since May Ella was treated as insane for aging.

Walking back to the car to head home, a gust of wind swept up just as I blew a large pink bubble in my gum, and I got to the house with a gob of it tangled in my hair. The first task of hunkering down for Bertha was Mom having to knead peanut butter into my scalp, pulling the bits of sticky, chewed gum from strands of my hair as the local news aired from the living room, hoping to get done before the lights went out. Bertha was expected to come ashore as a category two, which did not seem like too much to worry about. "Go upstairs and wash your hair again and then fill the bathtub with water. You remember what happened during Hugo," Mom reminded us about the tap water. Not so bad, considering the catastrophes of others. We lost power but not so much as a tree.

The sky was gray with Bertha when I woke up the next morning. This seemed like just the right kind of hurricane. Strong enough to be interesting, but too weak to do much damage. Maybe he just wanted something to think about besides his failing marriage, but Dad seemed happier than he had been. After breakfast, he set up a card table next to the front door with a view of the window, with a battery-powered radio and a deck of cards ready to shuffle. It had been a long time since we'd played gin. The rain started to fall. The wind became steady, blowing harder and harder throughout the day. By lunchtime, the rain had turned sideways and we were all out on the porch watching leaves and limbs tugged through the air, caught on something we couldn't see. Mom brought blankets to wrap around us. The sustained winds made the wet July day feel winter-cold. We watched a group of seagulls try to fly against the wind. They were stuck at a fixed point in the sky, flapping without moving forward and looking slightly ridiculous as gusts fanned out their feathers and butted their heads.

Inspired, my dad got up from his rocking chair, stepped off the front porch, and walked out into the gale. He looked up at the sky, apparently satisfied, and yelled for me and my brothers to join him. "Come on!" We looked at one another and bounded off the porch, leaving the blankets slumped on the rocking chairs and running into the rain. The wind pushed against us, and the drops of rain bore into my skin. "This is a game I played with my brothers," he said, and explained the rules. You have to face the wind head-on, and the last person standing after everyone else has been blown down wins. I could barely hear my own laughter over the roar of the wind.

When my brothers got back to their feet, our dad

had reappeared with a kite from the garage. My mom looked down from the porch, wrapped in blankets and with Jared on her hip, and my dad released the green diamond-shaped kite. "Mark, be careful! Watch out for lightning!" she had to scream, her voice cracking. She looked like she was crying, though it was impossible to tell with the rain. But the sound of my mother's heart breaking was louder than the freight-train sounds of the storm. Even now I hate the sound of my own voice cracking when I cry, when the tears come like the tor-rents of rain that fall for hours or days until the winds fizzle and the sky clears blue again and what's left is only a tropical storm the next state over and fallen trees in the backyard, if you're lucky. Because it sounds just like hers that day on the porch watching the kite buck and whirl in the sky. The pop of green flew through the gray sky, past the seagulls, who were still struggling. It was the same green as the stone on my mother's engagement ring, which she was not wearing anymore, and the kite blew away, disappearing into the sea or the sky or the past forever.

Late in the afternoon, the kite long gone and the rain just drizzle, Dad grew restless. "I'm gonna go see what the neighborhood looks like," he announced, and I volunteered to go too. We got in the little silver se-dan and drove along empty neighborhood streets and then turned onto the highway, also empty, taking in the damage. Some billboards had blown over and pine trees were either bending or snapped in half, but overall there wasn't the devastation I remembered from Hugo. Homes stood their ground and there was little storm surge, certainly not half a mile inland. All the video-rental shops, grocery stores, and fireworks outlets were shuttered, so it was a surprise to come across a Chinese restaurant in a strip mall with the neon OPEN sign lit up. We pulled in, and the family who ran the place seemed as nonplussed as my dad. They'd kept everything running on their generator after the power went out. We headed back to the house with cartons of Chinese food, delighted at the fun of our unlikely discovery. In the hour that we had been gone, though, a roadblock had been set up across the highway, just before our neighborhood. "No, sir," said the officer, unmoved. "We ain't lettin' nobody back in." We parked the car at a nearby fireworks outlet and, angry and soaking, lugged our bags of takeout, no longer a treat but a liability, through soaking pine forest, in freezing silence, as if criminals in our own home, and come to think of it, it was probably an offense to cross the barrier that had been set up. We might have been hungry looters, after all.

The wind was waning and summer warmth should have been returning with us, but our house had kept its unseasonable chill. The inconvenience of hauling noodles and stir-fry had dampened the mood, and Mom had already locked herself in her bedroom for the night. This was not what I had in mind, when I'd thought to offer our barroom mermaid to the ocean. I was too young still to understand the relief that came with endings, and kept from me was the gravity of my parents' money problems. Still saddled with medical debt from the emergency of Mom's last pregnancy, owing thousands of dollars in rent on the restaurant to Uncle Herman, who was nearly as stingy as Granddaddy, and nearing foreclosure, the only option was to beg for help from Grandpa. As generous as Granddaddy was greedy, he would not give as freely as he might once have. In paying off the little blue house in Little River, he gave the condition that we leave Myrtle Beach for good and move to Charlotte. If he was not a miser with his money, he knew how to make a deal. That was how he got rich in the first place. The strings he tied to his money reflected his own selfishness, moving his favorite child and her family close to him. Though I did not know the details yet, such offers imparted the sense that no matter how bad things got, there would always be a safety net in his outstretched hands, which also held his checkbook.

By the time the storms got up to the Fs, in September of that year, we would be living down at Nana's house. We sold the blue house to pay off the bank, or rather, my grandpa paid off the bank to stop the foreclosure. F for Fran, for foreclosure, for failing. What little we kept from our house ended up in a storage unit on the Little River side of the swing bridge. Hurricane Fran was forecast to hit Myrtle Beach dead-on as a category four, and for the first time, we evacuated. We packed up the alien-green minivan and drove to the safety of Grandpa's house, leaving Dad behind at Nana's house. They could tell Fran would wobble north at the last minute, as it did, and hit North Carolina harder than the Low Country. Fran remains the last strong storm to come ashore in the Carolinas, the last one to be ranked officially devastating, and our storage unit in Little River flooded to the rafters. The tide claimed what little was left of our family life.

From the library at school, I filled out and mailed applications to better-looking schools in Charlotte. I hoped I would learn more than I had been. In my eighth-grade history class, for instance, we spent afternoons learning the words to the county fight song. "It's 'Horry' not 'Whore-y,'" the chorus counters what must have been a common misconception. We had to pretend to be among the enslaved Africans on a rice plantation after the annual field trip to Brookgreen Gardens. That year was the last for the old school building. A newly constructed one was about to open next door, and on a warm spring day at the very end of the year, the students showed up ready for Field Day, only to be lined up side-by-side in a chain hundreds of kids long. Under open sun, we passed the library books from the old building to the new one. I was not sorry to be leaving.

Since this is the line in the road where I become a tourist in my own hometown, it's a good time to expand here on Myrtle Beach's becoming a tourist town to begin with. There is a good chance that you have been there and molded your own sandcastle from a yellow plastic tub as your mother misted you with a greasy spritz of coconut oil, or if you were fairer, slathered you with white SPF thick as shortening. That you have picked sandspurs out of your heels and stuffed yourself to bursting with popcorn shrimp and deep-fried flounder. If you have been there for spring break, well, your secrets are safe with me. I have better things to do than guess how many shots you've thrown back on a fake ID, or divine a future from the tan lines left fading across your back. They work truer than the palm, I believe.

Myrtle Beach, you will remember, had been renamed by the richest lady in the county, though by now most of the wax myrtle bushes are long pulled from the sand for motel parking. If you are curious about what the coast looked like then, try the Meher Baba ashram, as it is an officially designated wildlife sanctuary where humans may apply for brief refuge among the migratory herons of blue or white and nesting loggerhead sea turtles. I have long wished to glimpse them, these hatchlings like beating hearts in suits of armor who, on fluttering wings, emerge from where they were buried at the edge of life to shuffle over sand to the ocean that scoops them up and out to sea. What I have seen are the lines tracing their first moments left across moonlit sand toward the hem of high tide.

Toward the end of that hurricane summer in 1996, Dad drove past motels with names like Windsurfer, Windjammer, Sea Gypsy and Sea Mist, the Captain's Quarters and Paradise Resort, Camelot by the Sea and the Caravelle, past the Tropical Seas, and then the Mermaid Inn to move up to Emerald Isle, a sleepy family vacation town on the Outer Banks where he worked in Uncle Leslie's construction company. Working was better than rehab, which we could not have afforded, anyway, and Mom was expected in Charlotte. We would finish the school year living at Nana's house, and Mom was going to be Grandpa's secretary at Carolina Time, enlisted into the family business of clockmaking. Once the construction job was over, Grandpa planned for Dad to manage a long-term parking lot next to the Charlotte airport that Grandpa owned, parking the cars of people on their way to see the world. We were all to live with him and his house ghost, Harvey.

I took the prospect of leaving Myrtle Beach with more grace than my parents or brothers, though as naivety suffers more for its eagerness, I would be no different in my desire to return. Calls began coming in for Mom at Nana's house. Schools with fancy names, Country Days and Latin Days and Christian Days, left messages requesting our summer schedule. My eyes widened with the guilty conscience of a kid just busted for secret schemes, but even more in disbelief that I was not going to be trapped after all. Education I had always known was my way out of town.

Beating all the kids who pulled my hair and pushed me in hallways, who emptied my book bag and kicked over my desks, in test scores and G.P.A. felt pretty good, though. In a science class my senior year, we had to construct a rocket with a parachute, and the team whose model took the longest to float down won. After seeing my assigned partner's terrible calculus, I politely told him, as I imagined Nana might do, that he had not to worry about one thing. I would do it all. As all women learn, just doing the work yourself saves you the trouble of arguing with men who know less than you. Watching my rocket float down as lazy as an angel, and seeing the face of a regular bully crinkle in with sour petulance, well, it is a memory that buoys me still.

When I was sent home for wearing my best overalls to this fancy private school, I cried waiting for Grandpa to pick me up. He took me home and told me of the insults thrown at him for never having shoes at school. I knew that he understood without pandering to my tears. He recognized an outsider like himself. The shared wonder of education connected us further, and I suppose it was that day that I knew he would be my only friend in high school. I had wanted out of Myrtle Beach, but the confidence to cross a highway and own a lazy river was left back in the tangled limbs of marshside oaks. Dad left Charlotte for Nashville, as soon as he could, and we didn't hear from him for a long time. Months without calls turned into years without seeing him. On his way out of town, leaving his family behind, Dad stopped by Lebo's Country Western Store and bought a new cowboy hat and boots that he still has today. A dream can resurrect as easily as a memory, like a ghost you thought you'd gotten rid of, and for a while he was a ghost to us, as we were a memory for him. Untangling yourself from someone else's dreams takes all the liquor and lyrics you've got, and he left knowing that Grandpa would take care of us better than he could at the time.

"You ever hear from Mark?" Grandpa would ask tentatively but regularly through my years of high school and into college, and I would only shake my head no. I trusted him, but also wanted to impress him. Didn't want Dad to suffer in the eyes of a man I knew he admired, too.

"Nana, why can't he just call?" I could ask her over the phone without fear, and let her see I also knew that my parents were still stuck in their rhythms of fighting and making up and trying to hide it, even though they were divorced by then.

"I don't know, baby. He's always had the devil in him," she said. "Every night, it takes me two hours to say my prayers for my boys. And most of that time is spent on your daddy."

A decade or so later, Dad called me up at two a.m. He sounded surprised I picked up, and I could tell he was drunk and in tears. My heart, in daylight angry and embittered at his absence, under moonlight cracked open under the transmission of his pain. "Was I a good father?" he whispered, not bothering to hide his weeping. It was not the moment then to say that he was, back when I knew him. It had been so long since I had known him as a young man with the sunshine of youth who would mend childhood scrapes with stories and card games.

As I longed to do then but could not, I will skip over
the rest of high school. The only memory that tempts
symbolism is of the time Mom found a copperhead
coiled in the bathroom at Grandpa's house. I woke to
screams in the middle of the night caused not by Harvey,
whose haunting we by then were used to and thought
so little of as to stop mentioning it to one another, hallway footsteps and pocket doors sliding open and shut.
My brother Jason got the worst of it one night alone
in the house, when the clanging of pots and pans, the
slamming of kitchen cabinet doors drove him outside. A
friend found him waiting to be picked up in the driveway wearing only his underwear. Animal control came
to remove the copperhead, suggesting we might have a
nest in the ventilation, but we never encountered another
inside the house. In college, I could not believe how little most of my fellow undergraduates cared to be there,
how they took their platinum education for granted. The
school I'd chosen, with a monster for a mascot, was just
like the high school I attended. Beautiful and privileged
and full of young people who didn't realize their luck.
Grandpa was paying for it all, of course, and would follow the reading list for courses with me sometimes. Most
weekends, I'd make the two-hour drive to Charlotte to
spend time with him and my brothers. I spent half the
weekend with him at his office, where he'd catch up on
paperwork, and I made pocket money filing and cleaning up. We traded the same copy of *Homage to Catal-
onia* back and forth with notes in the margins for each

other. I mailed large-print copies of *Love in the Time of Cholera* to Nana, among the humid, high romances I had just discovered that I loved. Books were saving me, as they always did. I sent her *One Hundred Years of Solitude* after that. Didn't your grandparents ever say that time speeds up as you get older? "Sometimes I look in the mirror, and I don't know who that old woman is," Nana said to me more than once.

One early fall weekend, I drove to Charlotte, as I often did, to see Grandpa for a few days of work. I expected the following week's classes to be canceled. It was hurricane season, and it was plain to anybody who kept a map that Hurricane Ivan would sweep up from the gulf through the oaky quads of my college town. Ivan was an unusual storm that should have been called Lazarus. It circled over the entire southeast before returning to the Atlantic and making an unheard-of downward spiral back to Florida and into the Gulf of Mexico, where he was resurrected as a hurricane and made landfall for the second time. More elliptical in shape than the usual parabola across the page, if you are keeping a hurricane chart, as I have been taught to do.

I had been away from the coast long enough to misjudge the warnings.

Forgive this untruth. As we approach the last chapters, as pages wane to nothingness, I am tempted by swift absolution when I must confess to knowing what I was doing and then doing it anyway. Ivan was only a category one by then, weakened by its journey overland.

A storm of so little consequence, I thought there was no danger in proceeding as normal. I repacked the car and drove back to college through the rain. I had thought that it would be fine, but the rain was heavier than I anticipated, and for the first time in a hurricane, I felt scared. The car buzzed over patches of hydroplaning I could not see. There was no witch protecting us with a wave of her fingers. I thought of Uncle Keith. Yes, here, as we approach our own ending, we find out what happened, as far as we know ourselves. Last we left off, he was on the lam, as they say, and only Uncle Jack knew his whereabouts. The FBI and the drug cartels or the mob or all three were rumored to have been looking for him, according to family stories, and eventually they found him by following Jack. They were in Florida, of course, where folks go to bask in their misbehavior, even in hiding. Jack got off a plane in Miami and was shot down on the tarmac. "He's still got the scars," Dad said recently, as these stories are told over and over, and I let Dad's slip of tense slide, because Uncle Jack has been dead of cancer for years now. But back down in Florida, Keith and his wife were killed by an eighteen-wheeler, a log truck stacked with pines. Were they struck just as my parents were? Did they see the driver's face? The other cars getting sucked under the belly? I thought of my parents and of my great-uncle and his wife. The driving was very bad in the hurricane, and in a fit of anxiety I could only recall disasters. As the story goes in our family, before the local highway patrol could get to the accident, the FBI had already roped off the scene, and it is all-around suspicious. This is how the story of Uncle Keith ends, and it always begins with Dad or Les going, "Let me tell you about my uncle Keith." I got to school shaken and soaked. I walked to class avoiding flying tree limbs, only small ones, and got to the door to see that the university had canceled after all. Turning to rewalk the flooded path, my memories wandered farther, to wooden mermaids and the night of Hugo, to the Gray Man and to Alice Flagg just out of sight.

11

The Suckers List

"I GOT A GREAT IDEA, BUT I DON'T HAVE A LOT of money and I'm in trouble with the law." These are the words that brought the crook Denny Cerilli into our lives.

I can see it all now. Tall and white-haired. Described by newspapers as stylish and likable, as well as a con man. In the uniform of the men whose money he was so good at stealing. Collared polo shirt, wingtips of real Italian leather that fell off the back of a truck. Slacks of plaid or plain polyester with crease too prominent and waist too high. All the better for deep pockets, my dear.

He walked into my granddaddy's office on Twenty-ninth Avenue and laid out a presentation of such improbable grandiosity that it had to be well thought-out.

"Howdy, howdy," Granddaddy would've said as he extended his hand.

"Mr. Jones, they tell me you're the man to see in this town," this stranger would have appealed to his vanity as he looked around at the peach carpet, his couch striped in burgundy and hunter green. Golf trinkets and pictures given as Father's Day gifts lining the long tables of dark wood.

This is the part where we arrive finally at a moment of comeuppance. Denny was pushing a scam from top to bottom, and he called it the Carolina Amphitheater. This is the last scene where we see Granddaddy in a state of wealth and possibly a state of sanity.

How did he find my granddaddy? It used to be that when a bank refused a loan, they might recommend going to see somebody with large private funds. I think it more likely that Denny found his name on an official Suckers List, a directory of elderly, sick, or just plain gullible that circulates among scam artists.

His audacity made Denny a popular man in South Carolina, and like all con men, he picked up quick the language of the land. I have heard him called in tones of derision a carpetbagger by old Southern ladies, my nana included, for whom the mere approximation of profanity provoked a week of apologies. The only other person I've heard Nana take a cussword to is Uncle Mike. Denny had a vision, you see. A razzle-dazzle vision! An entertainment venue so grand, so majestic it would make every investor a millionaire ten times over. Right in the middle of Marion County, an hour and a half inland from Myrtle Beach and surrounded by two hours of swamp and farmland on all sides. He'd been arrested already for pulling the same scam, selling a town in Pennsylvania on a mountain amphitheater and lining his pockets with this small town's cash before skipping town. If anybody comes at you saying they've got a vision, best to keep on walking because the only future they've seen is the one where they have all your money. Granddaddy was already a millionaire when Denny showed up to his office, but greed is like Low Country quicksand, and once you've got your foot in, there's nothing to do but sink.

Dad had started making the rounds in Nashville by then, playing for tourists walking down Broadway on their way to the Ryman. Between busking in front of Tootsie's and small-time gigs, Dad found that he needed some company to occupy the time and space formerly filled with all the noise of four kids. He adopted a shaggy brown Newfoundland dog so big there followed a spate of bear sightings in front of the Nashville Coliseum. Dad named the dog Conway, letting the musicians of Music City think he was named after Conway Twitty, when he was named for the town where we were once a happy family. They are bred, these dogs, to rescue the drowning, to pull bodies back to shore when they are drifting under, too tired to go on. Dad could not refuse Granddaddy when he called him up in Nashville and asked for his help with the Amphitheater, even after all the abuse and put-downs. The transmission of fantasies passes as easily across those invisible conduits that pass along hurts. Escape is never a onetime deal.

Denny, as per his usual modus operandi, had declared himself in charge of getting the construction going, after Granddaddy had invested most of his money and talked his brothers and friends into investing their own. Denny blew into town promising to make everyone richer, and I picture him riding out in a Thunderbird like my great-granddaddy's, piles of cash in the back seat, bills sucked out and swirling in the wind of his French exit. He was a wanted man up north, wanted supposedly by both the mob and the U.S. Attorney's Office, like the stories about Uncle Keith. It is said that when the feds came down to Myrtle Beach offering him immunity for his scams in Pennsylvania or Lord knows what, he took it and then took off, which might have been his plan all along, if that is what happened. Granddaddy lost millions of dollars, and his best friend would die a broke man. He'd gotten all his brothers in on the deal, and they lost just about as much. Uncle Jack sued Granddaddy and was the only one who got his money back. Until just recently a billboard announcing the Carolina Amphitheater stood over an empty field in Marion, South Carolina, looming over the imagined ruins of the biggest stage in the state.

After the Amphitheater, Dad and his dog, Conway, went back to Nashville full-time. After gigging around town for a while, he landed regular shows at the Bluebird Café, which, if you don't know, is just about the

best place to make a name for yourself if you want to
break into songwriting big time. It's where all the young,
pretty faces looking for stardom go to find the words for
their voices. At the Bluebird, he sang stories about losing
the battle with alcohol and women's fingernails running
down his back. One night after a show, he drank in the
dawn with Waylon Jennings and Emmylou Harris. He
fell in with a new crew of outlaw country musicians and
was arrested once or twice. If Conway was in the car
when he got pulled over, he'd roll down the back window and let the dog stick his bear-size head over the side
of the car. The cop would usually jump back and shout,
"Shit, Mister. You got a grizzly in your truck?" And Dad
would plead, "Officer, you gotta let me back on the road.
I got a certified water rescue dog and we're on our way
to save somebody." It wasn't that much of a lie. Conway
had rescued him. All the while, down South there is, as
there has always been, fightin' and fussin', kissin' and
makin' up, kept secret from Grandpa and half-hidden
from me and my brothers. Dad's visits to Charlotte are
infrequent but the pattern remains unchanged: his truck
pulls into my mother's driveway for days or weeks, only
to disappear in the middle of the night without a word
of parting.

After a period of steady Bluebird round-robin nights
and Mom bailing him out of jail for a variety of vio-
lations, just enough to give him that outlaw finish, he
got an invitation to come see one of the most renowned
publishing houses on Music Row. He and Conway were

living in his truck at the time. He pulled into the office's parking lot, behind the quaint-looking Victorian converted house. Unshaven and hungover, he stripped down to his underwear in the parking lot to change into a better outfit. The secretary watched from behind pulled-back curtains as he pulled on his boots with the fanged snakes' heads on the toes, and she nearly wouldn't let him in the door. The publisher led him into a conference room with a long table in the middle and walls of guitars. He'd left his guitar in the truck and asked to borrow one off the wall, and started playing and couldn't stop. He played that guitar all afternoon and into the night, channeling the spirits it contained, not once getting up from the conference table. The publisher wouldn't let him leave without signing a contract, and I wonder if Dad thought about all those times Uncle Jack had held him hostage, too, as all day and all night he played his own songs on the guitar that wrote songs for Patsy Cline and "Take This Job and Shove It." The next morning, he left with a signed publishing contract and a promise to set him up to write with any writer he'd ever admired. Dad has made it through the door, and his house has yet to burn down. What a weight lifted from a back bent low when you are recognized for what you know you are supposed to do. When he used to say that Conway was famous in Nashville, he was saying that he was, and that when the publishing house hosted his fiftieth birthday a few years later, after writing and selling a string of hits, the publisher took down an urn from the mantel at the office on Music Row, stuck a finger into the ashes of a country-music legend, and drew a cross across my dad's forehead, a baptism that turned him into what he knew he was all along.

Let's take a breath on a moment of triumph. We will soon need our strength and must bask in the restorative powers of victory. Like pushpins in a hurricane map, I have left wobbling pins charting a path out of the South altogether, to study books and writing in New York.

One stormy spring about a decade later, when a new complex called the Swamp Fox Entertainment Complex stood where the Amphitheater would have, I walked down a wide, leafy Brooklyn block, skyscraper steel and brownstone separating me from a past that seemed a world away, when Mom called to say there had been an accident at Nana's house. Granddaddy had fallen some days ago and had either forgotten about his concussion and scalp cut wide open, or kept his injuries a secret. By the time Leslie happened to stop by and find his father also at home, he couldn't remember who he was even though he was driving back and forth between Nana's house and his office. He fell unconscious in the ambulance up to Myrtle Beach Hospital. When could I fly down?

Granddaddy had become obsessed with regaining his fortune since the Amphitheater, and had once even asked for my Social Security and bank account numbers. He knew a guy who could double whatever was in it. I held his hand and smiled while not knowing what to do, see-

ing him as not only the tyrant of my childhood, but newly
as a frail old man desperate to recover his self-worth,
which was always in his money. That was the most plau-
sible of his get-rich quick schemes. Where he found them
is still a mystery. There was the emerald mine in Italy
that needed investors to free hostage jewels owned by
the pope. A man from Texas had invented a machine
that cures cancer and kept it on an oil rig in the middle
of the ocean, he just needed a little money because the
government had covered it up and was after him, though
it was a sure investment. Then there was the earthworm
farm, which he could not explain properly but still elicits
wide eyes and head shakes. The car that runs on sand
instead of gasoline. In a newfound spirit of generosity, a
sign of his declining mental state, he was trying to spread
the wealth and get us to invest, too.

Dad picked me up from the airport, and on the ride
to Myrtle Beach Hospital, tried to prepare me for how
bad Granddaddy was. How he walked around for days
with such a head injury was both strange and bad for
the prognosis. They'd had to remove a part of his skull
to ease the pressure on his swollen brain. In the hospital
parking lot, the same one where he and Les waited for
their granddaddy to die, he pulled out a CD from the
console of his truck, and for the first time since we lived
in Conway, he played me his songs and asked what I
thought. A young singer who'd end up on the cover of
every gossip magazine in Walmart sang his words on a
demo called "The Devil in Me." I could think only of

Nana and her prayers. He had swiped her line and made it true. Granddaddy looked bad, tossing and turning, mumbling and groaning in pain. He'd spend six months in a rehab center after a recovery as mysterious as his fall. The first two weeks he was in the hospital, it didn't look like he'd make it. Even after his head wound healed, he refused to eat anything and the doctors had to insert a feeding tube.

His brothers, the two still living then, came by to check in on him. Wilbur was coming down the hallway headed for the room one afternoon, when Granddaddy, perhaps sensing the approach of his brother, started mumbling about hiding the moonshine in the trunk and jumping in the car. "Hit the gas," he said just as Wilbur walked in.

Wilbur paused in the doorway, looked at Granddaddy and then the nurses at their station behind him, as if afraid he'd been busted, and tiptoed backwards down the hallway without a word to us. Granddaddy murmured about being stuck in jail and about conquistadors who were stealing his gold. The spirit of Lucas Vázquez de Ayllón landed anew. One morning I was sitting next to his hospital bed. As Jared, a grown man now, and Leslie were chatting in the doorway, Granddaddy stiffened and opened his eyes. Asleep or delirious since my arrival, he grabbed my arm and looked at me. With a gaze as clear as the highest-proof moonshine, he whispered, "Nicole, let me die." He then dropped back into sleep.

Back at Nana's house, the family sat around her recliner trying to figure out how he fell. Nana had been to
the hospital every day, and acted always as a devastated
and worried wife ought to. We all hoped he'd be the first
to go, that she'd have a few years of freedom without his
nasty cruelties, delivered regularly and without provocation. Too frail to smack her around anymore, he hurt
her with unending insults and by banning her from their
bedroom, where there's a wall-size mirror next to the
sink in the bathroom. Les and Dad kept going over the
trail of blood found in his bathroom. Down the mirror
and on the carpet, broken glass from a little table that
fell with him. "There's nothing for him to trip on back
there," I heard Les posit, and suddenly I imagined Nana,
herself pushed too far after sixty years, pushing him
down and then walking away. And I wanted her to have.

My brothers and I have a pact: we'll never let any
one of us get sent to a hospital in South Carolina, even
if it means wrestling a gurney away from an EMT. I
advise you, elicit the same promise from those you care
about. We're not quite done with Myrtle Beach hospi-
tals, I am afraid. When I returned to New York after
a week in Myrtle Beach preparing myself for his death,
which against the odds didn't occur then, I saw my
healer in the railroad apartment. I didn't know what to
make of Granddaddy's moment of lucidity. Had it even
happened? Though I didn't know what to make of this
woman's claims, I needed to talk about the fear in his
eyes, how scared he seemed, and my own fear in nobody

else having seen or heard him. "Yes, of course. He can tell you talk to ghosts," she said, as if asked the time. I paid her and never went back.

Riding the subway one morning on the way to work, I was jolted by a sudden stop and my cheek smacked hard into a metal wall. I tried my hardest not to cry, but tears of pain began to fall down my swelling cheek. By the time I reached the office where I spent hours correcting the spelling in cookbooks and science-fiction novels, my eye was nearly swollen shut underneath a glaze of tears. My black eye drew looks from strangers, sympathy and scorn, I imagined, and even to my friends, the truth sounded lame and false. I thought of my nana, and how just a few years before, surgery to relieve pain in her ear had left her with a black eye and hearing loss on the one side, which was not the intended outcome. I suggested we go out for breakfast when she was nearly recovered, the eye and cheek yellow instead of purple, to Aikel's or the Pancake House, or that we take a walk on the beach. Her refusal, unusually adamant, felt laced with shame. She must have known enough the looks of concern and judgment going about your day will get you with a black eye. What excuses did she use when she couldn't hide her bruises? Back in my apartment, I hoped again that Nana had pushed Granddaddy down.

He moved into a nursing home for a few months. I went down again to visit. Nana went to see him every day, ever dutiful. She brought his favorite pears and fruitcakes. Brought his mail and phone messages she had taken. Brought him clothes and magazines he asked for. One day, she walked in and noticed something she had not brought him.

"Ralph, are the nurses mixing up your laundry?"

"Jackie, why are you here, I told you not to come by today. Ain't nobody wants to see you here."

"What are you wearing?" She was mad now. The intuition of the wounded kicked in.

He had a standing date with F at the nursing home, and clothed himself in the things she brought for their reunions. From the car, Nana called Les in tears.

"What do you want me to do, Mama? I been telling you just like everybody else to divorce him."

"You know I can't do that."

"I don't see why not. I'll drive you down to the courthouse myself."

She brought him his mail the next day like all the others. Against some odds and wishes, Granddaddy recovered enough to return to Nana's house on Calhoun Road, by then truly her house, just as her grandchildren had always called it. After the failure of the Amphitheater, Granddaddy had to sign the house over to her ownership so his creditors wouldn't be able to claim it.

If you are from Beaufort, it is likely that you have heard the story of little Julia Legare. If she had been born in our century, she might have been a pageant queen with her breeding. Before she was just another affluent girl carried away by a mosquito bite, Julia was a child of her time, which was the early 1800s. From her home in

Edisto, south of Murrells Inlet, she learned her letters, went to church, embroidered Bible verses. Whatever it was that affluent young ladies did at that time. She might have had tea with Eliza Pinckney, the indigo grower. There would be no chores for her. Little schooling. Very little life at all, sadly. She was buried in the family mausoleum in Edisto Beach, which draws visitors even now. Tourists and teenagers, mostly. When the marble door to the mausoleum was opened after the next death in the family, more than a decade later by most accounts, the grieving family found the body of little Julia not in her grave but beside the door, which has never again been closed despite some effort. After trying to lock, dead-bolt, or otherwise chain the portal closed and finding it reopened in the daylight, the family gave up and just left it open for Julia to roam free as she likes, as free as any man living and the spirit of any woman dead.

From her rocking chair, Nana told me over and over the story of Alice, of the Flagg Flood, and many others. Read from her books on the coffee table and from memory. She told only one story about her granny, but it is a real gem among them. This is the granny who had fifteen children. Nana's mother, May Ella, was the mystical seventh, the first daughter who was herself heard to proclaim that she'd rather have a heart attack than another baby after her children were born, which is what she died from, after all. The favorite pastime of Granny, my great-great-grandmother, was sewing over and over a funeral shroud for herself. From whatever scraps of white fabric she could find, she made shroud after shroud. After completing each one, she'd ask one of her children or grandchildren what they thought about this one and then the next. No matter their reply, every time she undid the stitches and tore out the thread. May Ella worked at the Air Force Base during World War II and even brought her mother some yards of fine white parachute silk to be cut and recut, joined and torn open as she pleased. Once her children and grandchildren were grown, this was how she spent her days, waiting to wrap herself in white silk that must have been finer than whatever she was married in. I could take it to mean that she felt her work was done, her children born, alive, and grown, so what was there left for a woman to do but die. In some grief for this woman I didn't know, my heartbreak for a grandmother who obsessed over her grave clothes for decades, I want to see the possibility that this repetition was some final act of subversion. Here was a gift of luxury and selfishness just for herself. In the precision of stitches, some sense of control. She chose to wrap herself in a life of her own making.

It is neither as straightforward nor as metaphorical as I want. How can I heal all of these women, my grandmamas going back to one flood or another? It hardly matters which, there have been so many. A parable so perfect that Jesus could not have done it better than my nana. Maybe he did, but I confess that I have never read the good book and have no plans to in the future. I am choosing the stories from the mouths of women, some painted and some bare, and as far as I am concerned, their words are all the truer for the color. I am also putting off what I cannot bear to lose for good, and like a hurricane, I will change tack without warning.

The ghost of Theodosia Burr keeps me company in New York. She is seen in the finest translucent fabric descending in ethereal grace to earth via staircase, of all vehicles, in an old townhouse on Barrow Street in Greenwich Village. Women report their earrings pulled at by her, as if to say, Listen. Or, just, These would look better on me. Did you know some claim that Theodosia's ghost walks along the Grand Strand in search of her father? Rumors run amok, I say. If she is not by her husband in Brookgreen Gardens, and why would she be, what had she to keep her tied to Ocean Boulevard? I will keep Theodosia in New York, where her presence makes sense, where it follows the rules. That is not her walking up and down the beach of the Low Country enjoying the sun of a New Year's Day in a pink bikini top.

12
_____

The Gray Man

THERE IS ONE LAST GREAT HURRICANE WHOSE winds will blow through these pages. The Flagg Flood of 1893 is occasionally mistaken for the Mermaid Storm of 1881. Allow me to set the record straight. Yes, we are once again among the Flagg family, with one of Alice's brothers, in fact. Not Allard, the brute who sent her away from her lover and induced the attack of heartbreak that killed her, but Arthur, who has not long to live at the moment. In the book of folktales Nana kept on her coffee table, the one whose cover is laced with live oak limbs and drooping moss, the story is told as if from the perspective of the only survivor, Arthur's son Joshua Ward Flagg. The same Wards who claimed the most enslaved people in America before the Civil War. It was an

October Friday. A Friday the thirteenth, believe it or not, and the Flagg family had relocated to their oceanfront estate on Magnolia Beach, known today as Huntington Beach, near to their Pawley's Island home, to bear the final weeks of summery heat with the seaside breezes that kept the malarial mosquitos away. The strongest winds of the hurricane came in suddenly that morning following several days of storms. The sand and marsh were already soaked and ready to flood. The day the ocean and the creek embraced, that is what some still call the Flagg Flood, which is also deemed the Magnolia Beach Disaster in a newspaper account to mark its fortieth anniversary, in 1933. By the time the Flaggs realized they needed to reach higher ground, the marsh creek was too dangerous to cross and they were stuck. They spent some hours in their attic, before riding a piece of the roof to the top of a cedar tree where some of their servants clung. The winds are described as "sand-laden" that cut "flesh like sharp pieces of glass." A cousin called Allard was last seen holding his cat and floating away on the roof of the kitchen as his horse swam behind him. By one o'clock that afternoon, so said one of three survivors from the household, the sky was the perfect clear blue that I know myself and the sea lay calm and flat. Dr. Arthur, his wife, three of their children, and a handful of unlucky cousins visiting for the season were drowned along with hundreds of others. If only the Flaggs had heard that the Gray Man had been seen walking the beach of Pawley's Island.

In the Georgetown Museum, this unnamed family is quoted as believing the Gray Man saved their lives and protected their home. If I were writing that story, I would include a ring on a ribbon, like that of poor ghostly Alice Flagg, washing up among the debris, in perfect and mysterious, some might say vindictive, condition. In the graveyard at All Saints Episcopal, in the Flagg plot, be sure to find the memorial to the rest of the family since we have already visited the flat marble stone marked only ALICE that most tourists are so eager to spot. On a dirt-and-moss-covered obelisk, a lengthy inscription has been carved in loving memory of "those lost in the storm on October 13th, 1893." I have heard it told that Alice Flagg perished not from heartbreak or fever, but in the tidal wave that killed most of her family. As you and I know, such stories are flat wrong. She was looking for her ring decades before the storm of 1893.

In 2012, on the last day of summer, the season of disasters and catastrophes, my brother Jason called me first to say that Grandpa had a stroke and wasn't expected to live until morning. I stayed awake all night waiting for the predawn flight. I imagined conversations with him in my empty apartment. I whispered aloud, "Please don't go." And then, "If you have to go on your own adventure now, don't worry about me." The power went out just as my lips closed. It came back after a minute or more, but my alarm clock blinked the time in red like the plat-eyes I would be so scared to see in the woods at night. Jason called to say he was gone. I could only say "One thirty-two" over and over again, until my brother, through his own tears, whispered, "How did you know?" Had he dispatched Harvey or played the trick himself? We will all be ghosts one day, if we are lucky.

The airport in Charlotte was the last place I saw Grandpa alive, which seems the way it was supposed to be after a friendship started with the spin of a globe. He dropped me off, as he always did, and I flew back to New York, where I stayed after graduate school. He always picked me up when I returned as well, waiting just beyond the designated line to lift me up in a hug and spin me around with the joy of reunion, as he had done in his driveway so many times. He had been diagnosed with lung cancer my last year at graduate school in New York, after smoking since his second-grade teacher offered him a cigarette, and, as I had in college, I was returning to Charlotte most weekends to spend time with him. Our shared faith in the power of education was not in vain, it turned out. I landed a prestigious internship with ease, and was lucky enough to get writing and editing jobs right out of school. I got a callback for a job at a glossy magazine as we said our goodbyes, final it would turn out. "I knew you could do it." He picked me up off the curb and spun me around like I was five years old again, barefoot and beaming in his driveway.

I had not yet lost anyone important and did not know what to expect from grief. I did not expect, as I should have, to be helpless in the face of magical thinking, to find comfort in the logic of ghosts I had left in childhood. I heard his voice everywhere. It called to me at the oddest of times. I heard it first the day after he died. Mom was suddenly in charge of his business, Carolina Time, and had to account for the valuable things left behind. Less than twenty-four hours had passed, and there I was sitting at a round plastic table with Mom counting out foot-tall stacks of cash and taking an inventory of guns and jewels. It was as if a pirate's treasure chest had exploded. In silence, we counted out close to fifty thousand dollars and tallied up watches and diamond rings and rifles and Glocks. I heard my name spoken so clearly in his voice that I knocked my stack of bills to the floor in shock, jerking around expecting to meet his gaze. I heard his voice as clearly as I heard the footsteps of Harvey.

I felt alone with a grief heavy and new, adrift without his reassurances that I belonged wherever I chose. Without the blessing of belief and the reassurance of his experience, I could not strip the old feeling that I wore a costume. Dressed up to match the fellow commuters on crowded subways, the cloak of an educated professional was one I wore willingly and more easily than sequins and plastic tiaras. If I was not quite free of family patterns or ghosts from a region whose values I considered backward even before I realized it, no officer of the law of men could force me to turn around and return to a life of captivity. Friends encouraged me to have more fun and to forget after I abandoned them at bars without warning when I thought again that I had heard his voice saying my name and had to excuse myself mid-conversation. Was he calling to me from wherever he had traveled, or were the well-trodden footpaths of habit traced across my memory in our daily conversations simply starting to grow over unused? Would they stop if I painted my ceiling blue, and would I want them to? One forgettable day, they stopped.

With money that Mom inherited from Grandpa, she and Dad bought a farm near Nashville that they have filled with rescue llamas. Grandpa after death had blessed Mom with what she wanted back most, which was her marriage. Dad came to the funeral and has never strayed from her since. It's a red-stained log cabin, the Llama Farm my parents call it, with a baby grand piano and a wide porch on forty rolling acres. They let a neighbor graze his cows and horses on their land, and it feels there as if time moves slower and the heartbeat tremolos of Carolina wrens duet just as they did in Nana's backyard. There's only one llama left living now, down from six when they first started. Black snakes sun in zigzags over the wooden fence, and a couple of circus ponies are picked on by the horses. Old Conway died, but they now have two new dogs, Waylon and Loretta. The first spring they had the place, Dad found himself at midnight driving to his office in Nashville. It was burning down. On the news the next day, I watched firefighters in yellow hats and yellow coats hand Dad his guitars and songbooks as the flames danced around them in the porch until the sun came up. That's the thing about fire. It sucks up all the air in fantasies.

The logic of the Low Country came back to me, though I had been unaware of casting it aside. It was as if I had seen the Lands End Light, the light that appears floating in the road outside Beaufort. There are claims that it is a car, or the ghost of a car long crashed. I prefer the story that it is a hag, and if you see it you are blessed. Now conditions are right for seeing a real ghost. For telling his story. A disaster both natural and catastrophic looms. I have spotted a man, I think, but I can see straight through him. His blurry form walks between the sand and clouds on the beach at Pawley's Island and leaves behind no footprints. It is enough to know after seeing the Gray Man that you have been saved for something.

Before he was a ghost who wandered our beaches to warn of dangerous hurricanes on the way, the Gray Man was one of the Swamp Fox's soldiers. He was dispatched from the service of George Washington, on his way home to Pawley's Island, a lovely town between Myrtle Beach and Charleston, to reunite with a beautiful lover, when he fell into quicksand in the swamps of Marion and died. After receiving the news, this heartbroken lady took a walk along the beach in front of her home, and though she knew him to be dead, her beloved soldier appeared in front of her eyes and told her that she and her family must flee the coast. There was a hurricane coming. They left and survived a great storm, while the whole island was swallowed by storm surge. No home was left standing when the water receded except for theirs.

Or maybe he was the owner of a seaside inn whose life and livelihood were lost in a storm and who now returns to warn those listening.

He is sometimes said to be the spirit of Blackbeard himself, either not yet finished scaring the coast, or atoning for the havoc he raged on the very shores he presently saves.

Pick whichever story suits you.

Do ghosts wait on us, as we so desperately look for them? "Life is about creating memories," Grandpa used to say. Somewhere on some astral-plane space there is a version of all of this where Mom and Dad are not hit by that Mack truck, I'm meeting Grandpa for a drink tonight, and Nana is rocking on her porch swing, a great-grandbaby cooing in the nook of her neck, as she sings, "You are my sunshine, my only sunshine." When I need to talk to the dead these days, I take out the sweaters that smell like them, swiped from bureaus and the same hallway closet, where, after a funeral, a piece of curled-up notebook paper with a love song written on its faded lines was excavated alongside a matchbook from Drunken Jack's in a jewelry box found by accident in a closet at Nana's house.

13

Nana's House

ON THE LIVING-ROOM WALL AT THE LLAMA Farm, Mom has hung Dad's Grammy nomination on the wall. Best Country Music Song stands in gold next to his name. It's bigger than you'd think it'd be with the frame and its trimmings. The certificate hangs next to a picture of the two of them on the red carpet, walking into their sacred ceremony dressed in sparkles and satin. Finally they are where they always dreamed of being. Mom's had her hair shaped in hot-roller curls like how she did mine for pageants, and she's wearing a glittering beaded gown that brings out her green eyes. She looks as happy as I've ever seen her, and Dad looks slightly disbelieving in his tux. He brought a Stetson but left it back in the hotel room, and though he didn't end up winning the

Grammy that night, I know he's got a scribbled speech in his pocket that starts out, "I'm just a country boy from South Carolina with a sixth-grade education." I have seen him practice for the next time at the wheel of a new, paid-for pickup truck with a red plastic cup in one hand and conducting his music at full, exuberant volume with the other. His fingers move across what is visible to him, just as they did when he saw Whiskey Jones up on a marquee above King's Highway.

On Christmas Eve of 2016, a year that seemed to start out so joyfully as my parents walked the red carpet at the awards ceremony, Nana was taken to Myrtle Beach Hospital for a minor something. Do not worry, the doctors and nurses said, and we believed them. If one of us had insisted on staying after visiting hours, would she still have been given the medicine by mistake that slowed down her heart until it stopped beating? The heart is a muscle that remembers just like any other. Hers was shocked back to beating, but my nana's didn't come back with its pattern and she lay in a coma from Christmas Day until New Year's Eve. We tried to wake her, stroking her curves as familiar as the sand dunes across King's Highway and watching her feet tap to time as if she were in her rocking recliner waiting for the phone to ring or the patio door to open. "Where do you think she is right now? Is she a little girl again?" Dad asked this as we sat on either side of her bed, each holding a hand. Her eyes opened at times, still as bright and serene as the haint blue looking down on the Low Country, as if her

eyes were the sky itself. I have come to wonder if the fail-
ings of South Carolina medicine was the Lord's work.
After I landed in Myrtle Beach the day after her heart
attack, still hoping Nana would wake up, I was waiting
on the curb for Ralph Howard and Jason to pick me up,
when Jared called. Had I heard yet that our cousin Chris
was dead? That, in fact, Nana's heart had stopped at the
same time that Chris had died of a heroin overdose in
the last hours of Christmas Day.

We removed the life support after a week, feeling that she had been saved from a life without all of
her grandchildren. The designated morning, someone
brought Uncle Mike up to the hospital and wheeled him
into the room. His face was powdered white with what
Granddaddy had called Coca-Cola, and though Leslie
had tried to wipe it all off, enough had made it up his
nose and into his mouth so that, while relatives shuffled
in and out to say their final goodbyes to Nana, he went
between crying out, "She's a saint, my mother, a saint!"
and slapping the backsides of nurses and asking for their
phone numbers, until some family member drove him
home, to the Back House at Nana's. It was hard to chas-
tise him then. Nobody was in the mood, and he had lost
doubly. Before Mike could be notified of Chris's death a
week earlier, someone had posted the news online. Small
towns and all that. An EMT or his parole officer knew
someone who knew someone who couldn't keep their
mouth shut, and Mom saw the news of her nephew's
death on a social media page. On the way to Myrtle

Beach from Nashville, Dad called Mike to see how his
older brother was taking the blow, only to find out that
nobody had bothered to tell him yet, that he had in fact
broken the news, driving several highway exits' length of
confused silence that erupted into his brother's wailing.
Mike began planning an elaborate funeral for his son, to
whom he hadn't spoken in several years, not since Chris
had walked into the Back House and stolen the television off the wall. Mike called everyone he knew and
those he used to know in Myrtle Beach to invite them
to a gaudy and expensive funeral service he arranged.
Within just a few hours, he had put out an announce-
ment in the newspaper, ordered thousands of dollars' of
flowers, and had Chris's body transferred from Florence,
where he'd been paroled from jail for the holiday and
had been staying with his mother, all without her notice.
Chris's mom called up Uncle Leslie in as calm a state as
a grieving mother could manage, wondering what we
were doing transferring her son's body to Myrtle Beach
and planning a service without her, filled with people
Chris hated in a place that drove him to the needle? And
not knowing anything about it, Les could only apologize and call the funeral home to have Chris's body sent
back to his mother. I would never have predicted that
Chris would be the one who wandered up and down the
Grand Strand after death.

    After Mike was driven back to Nana's house, Les-
lie let go. "If I thought that I could get away with it,
I'd dump Mike off the end of Myrtle Beach Pier. Good

Lord, I think he might outlive us all." He sat down next to the window that overlooked the parking lot of Myrtle Beach Hospital, where he and Dad waited for their own granddaddy Harvey to die decades before.

"Damn, ain't it the truth. In that case, I might just throw Mike and his wheelchair in the back of my truck and drop him off at your house on my way out of town," Dad said.

"You do that and I'm gonna come back and haunt you," Les returned, and we all laughed, nobody saying but everybody smiling at the strange twist in their story. Mike and Granddaddy would be stuck sharing a roof alone. "It'll be a ghost town over there without Jackie," Les continued, trying to fill the silence. Except for the con men and charlatans pitching their latest scheme to Granddaddy, who didn't realize that he no longer controlled his finances, it will be, I think.

When it felt as if we were in her living room, telling stories with her rocking in her recliner, Nana let go a final ragged breath and her heart stopped for the last time surrounded by the voices and stories of her making. She was eased out of the world on a morphine drip, nearly the same as Chris had been. Mingled with our grief over Nana was renewed anger at Granddaddy. Though Nana tried to give Chris love and stability, with Granddaddy's strange and sad hatred directed at him, it is no wonder that my cousin chose the muggy, vengeful bliss of one drug and then another until he became a heroin addict. "She deserved better," Les said finally, before walking down to the parking lot, where my brothers and cousin Ralph Howard waited, not wanting to be in the room. Soon enough everybody else was in their cars. Heads on steering wheels, hands on packs of cigarettes, faces wet. As I am in charge of the story now, I record here for the future to note that none of us returned to the parking lot of Myrtle Beach Hospital ever again. We went back to Nana's house, where we, like children again, snuck into her old bedroom, and each chose one of the enameled lockets of perfume she collected. Standing in a circle, we held them aloft, my brothers, cousins, and I, and summoned her memory and the memory of the cousin who was missing as the scent of her surrounded us, connecting us not to any cartoon superhero as we had pretended and practiced, but to her spirit.

Nana's favorite Bible verse was the one about the virtuous wife. Her worth is far above rubies, and her husband shall never want. Just as I wonder sometimes if she finally snapped and pushed Granddaddy down to open up his head those years ago, I wonder if knowing these lines would be read to Granddaddy over her body was a slice of revenge on a husband who was far less virtuous. Only once did she ever express her anger over any part of her marriage in front of her grandchildren. Ralph Howard had driven with Jared and Jason to pick Nana up from her house, so that she could spend a day down in Murrells Inlet with us. They were backing out of her driveway and saw a car narrowly miss a pedestrian when she said, "You know, one day I saw that woman F coming out of the store, while I was waitin' for a parkin' space, and I had the urge to hit the gas pedal and run her down," as my brothers openmouthed and wide-eyed turned to look at each other, as if to cheer her on. "I don't like to hate anybody, but I sure as the devil hate her." She let it drop there, perhaps embarrassed at expressing a lifetime of stifled rage. Instead of silence or shock, the boys told her that they would have understood and held her blameless if she had run over her rival. I watched them all fall out of the car in loving laughter, my brothers and cousin lifting her from the car and up to the porch to watch the ocean for what would be the last time in life. It was quite a scene, three young men holding on their shoulders a glamorous blonde in movie-star sunglasses in a wheelchair, as if supporting a gilded palanquin in humble supplication.

She'd been sleeping in the Doll Room for years, kicked out of the marital bed. After the memorial service, I went in wondering if I'd hear her there, as I had unexpectedly heard my grandpa's voice. The blankets on one side of the bed were pulled back, where she'd stood up from sleep for the last time, and the other was covered with piles of her romance novels, where a lover might have lain. "I know you're not real girly," her words came to mind, but I knew they were remembered, not heard. "I don't know what you'll do with all these dolls." The doll collection remains as it ever was, encased in glass and untouched. I still don't know what to do with them, as she predicted, these emblems of her imagination, tokens of freedom, of other lives she could have lived had she been allowed. What would my voice sound like without her to direct the compass of my drawl? I wasn't sure, but I knew I wouldn't hear her voice calling to me as Grandpa's had. In the only dream I have had of her since she died, she is sitting on her couch in her house, next to her sister, Sue, and across from their mother, May Ella. Bathed in light, they are all young and happily chatting as they did in life from those very spots. As I was sure my grandpa had died with the unfinished business of some ghosts, I knew Nana had done what she set out to do in life. She'd made her grandchildren love her better than anything. She deserved better, but she gave away the best of anything she ever got.

A notebook filled with lifetimes of my family's stories was stolen from my car in a parking lot before Nana's death, and for months, I could not look at the white of paper without feeling her leave me again. She was the keeper of family stories. "I'm the matriarch," she asserted with a defiant pride, sure of her place at the head of a family that had belittled not just her, but all of its women, as if willing a world of women with power. Men have always been credited with the stories women kept alive. In returning to this place I had let go of, I would make her ghost not a lovesick or angry one as I'd learned the ghosts of women to be, but as the loving beacon I knew in life. What healers and psychics could not bring back after my first real experience with grief, I must do for myself.

Here, for the last time, I must take back my words. It is all more complicated than that. How can I heal all these women, my kith and kin, these mothers and grandmothers, much less myself, when I see now that I have been living out their eternal fates as if a ghost myself even as I try to write them into freer lives after death? I am little Julia Legare, who nightly forces open the doors between death and memory. I am the Lady in White, who plunges over and over into ocean waves to save not one body but generations under full moons reflected up and down the coast. Like Alice Flagg of the Hermitage I wear a gold ring on a chain around my neck to keep close the love of someone gone. With a silent clasp, on the morning of New Year's Day, I hooked one circle through another and walked once more across King's Highway from Nana's House, over Ocean Boulevard, beyond the boardwalk to the beach where I looked and looked until I found her between the dunes wearing on her finger the ring that I had around my neck.

Every Sunday, Nana told me that she wished she could follow me around for a day, to see what my life living somewhere else was like. One Sunday when Jared happened to be visiting her, we turned our phones on to video chat, and I walked her through my apartment, around my neighborhood, past subway entrances, doing laps around the park, telling her about my days in the city, how I had been apple picking the day before. "Ain't it a miracle," she declared, and at first, I thought she meant the technology.

If only I had the same skill with time as Grandpa, who could catch and move its hands at will over clock faces. Nana used to sneak barefoot to the clock, her mother's wedding present, on their family's mantel and wind back the hands to give her and her sister a little more time to play under the moon. If only I could reclaim the superstitions and stories passed on to me from fear and remake them as I would see the daughters of the Low Country. As free to be, to come and go, as they are to breathe. I could befriend the ghosts that wander the highway or find themselves lingering on the beach.

On the drive to the airport leaving one last time, I passed the oaks that hide the rice and indigo plantations now covered in sculpture and fairy lights in the shape of butterflies. The site where my great-grandmother ran her gambling parlor out of the gas station. The water park where my brothers and cousins and I splashed and warred with runes painted in neon zinc across our cheeks. The seafood joints, the motels and hotels, the lazy rivers and mini-golf courses. The vacant lot where the Pavilion used to stand before it was torn down for no good reason. The road that turns off King's Highway and leads to the swing bridge in Socastee. I think of my nana's favorite way to say goodbye as we reach the cemetery where we buried her yesterday, or a lifetime ago, under the name that is hers and mine. See you later, alligator, she liked to say with a wave in a lilting invitation for me to finish. Instead of holding my breath, I breathe her in and remember. After 'while, crocodile.

Acknowledgments

THANK YOU TO MY EDITOR, MEGHA MAJUMDAR, whose brilliance, grace, and generosity continue to amaze and humble. For the time and care you've put into this work, I will never be able to thank you enough. Here I will try once more, with deepest love: thank you.

Thank you to Catapult and the most wonderful team: Robin Billardello, Nicole Caputo, Wah-Ming Chang, Jordan Koluch, Alisha Gorder, Megan Fishmann, Rachel Fershleiser, Katie Boland, Samm Saxby, Laura Gonzalez, Dustin Kurtz. Your support and work on this book has meant the world.

Endless gratitude and love to my agent, Stephanie Delman, who reached out just as I was ready to give up. Your encouragement and belief in the vision I had for this book kept me going, and I am marvelously lucky to know you and to have you on my team. For anyone on the verge of giving up, keep going.

Thank you to my family, especially to Mom and Dad for your love and generosity—much of this book was written at a folding table in their storage closet. Thank you to Uncle Leslie and Robyn for all of your love and support, for the telling and retelling of family stories, for help with research. Thank you to my brothers: Justin, Jason, and Jared. My gratitude to Joanne Gaines for the love, care, and devotion to my nana over her lifetime.

Thank you to my friends, to my first readers, and to anybody who has offered kindness and help along the way. I am indebted and think with gratitude of you often: Gillian Jones, Marie Masson, Sara Lieber Green, Krishna and Emma Andavolu, Ryann Liebenthal, Angelina Fanous, Sophia Efthimiatou, Iza Wojciechowska (who doubles as proofreader), Ray Dademo, Katie Bachner, Ross Simonini, James Yeh, Liz Tingue, Hilary Leichter, Pat and Harriet Carrier, Leigh Black, Lis Harris, Ellis Jones, Ed Park, Dewitt Henry.

Thank you to readers and to independent bookstores.

Thank you to my dog, Juno, best good girl, squirrel huntress, and fastest pup at the dog park. Your goofy, bossy love makes everything better. And to Ben, whose unfailing support has made everything possible.

© Sylvie Rosokoff

J. NICOLE JONES received her MFA
in creative nonfiction from Columbia University and has held editorial positions at
VICE and *Vanity Fair.* She is the author of
The Witches of Bellinas.